RIBCHESTER EXCAVATIONS

Part 2

Excavations in the Civil Settlement

1968-1980

A. Structures

Editors:

B.J.N.Edwards   P.V.Webster

With Contributions By:

G.D.B.Jones, A.C.H.Olivier,

R.C.Turner, J.H.S.Witherington.

UNIVERSITY COLLEGE, CARDIFF,

DEPARTMENT OF

EXTRA-MURAL STUDIES

1987

ISBN   0 946045 30 5

Copyright: The Authors 1987.

Produced by the Archaeology Research Fund of the Department of
Extra-Mural Studies, University College, Cardiff with the aid of a
grant from the Historic Buildings & Monuments Commission (England).

Enquiries concerning the purchase of this volume should be made to:

The Administrative Officer,
Department of Extra-Mural Studies
University College
38 Park Place
CARDIFF CF1 3BB

Or:

The County Archaeologist
Lancashire Record Office
Bow Lane
PRESTON PR1 2RE

LIST OF CONTENTS

LIST OF ILLUSTRATIONS

PREFACE

This is the second of a several-part publication of recent excavations at Ribchester. Our reasons for adopting this format have been outlined in the earlier part (Edwards & Webster 1985; see Bibliography, this volume p.127 ff.). Also stated in the earlier part is our debt to many individuals and organisations both in Ribchester and elsewhere. Our debt to them is no less for simply being reiterated here.

This part contains reports on all but one of the sites excavated within the civil settlement at Ribchester between the years 1968 and 1980. The single exception is the Bath-house where lack of finance has so far prevented post-excavation work. It is intended to be read alongside Part 3 which will contain the pottery and coins (i.e. the major dating evidence). A later part will contain details of other finds from these sites.

As was the case with excavations published in Part 1, the excavations published here overlap the general change-over from imperial to metric measurement on excavations. As stated in the earlier part, we have resisted the temptation to convert all imperial measurements as we feel that this imparts a spurious precision to metric measurements thus achieved. Instead measurements throughout will be given in their original units and approximate equivalents will be given where this seems desirable.

Post-excavation work on the sites reported upon in Chapters 3, 6 and 8 were undertaken in facilities kindly made available by the Department of Classics and Archaeology at the University of Lancaster and with the aid of grants from the Department of the Environment. Work towards Chapter 4 and the completion of Chapter 3 have been undertaken in the Cumbria and Lancashire Archaeological Unit with the aid of grants from the Historic Buildings and Monuments Commission. The work of editing has also been eased considerably by financial aid from the Commission. The production of final copy has been split between the Unit and the Department of Extra-Mural Studies, University College, Cardiff. We are grateful to both these bodies and to the Lancashire Record Office for considerable help during the preparation of this series.

We have attempted to keep the format of this part as similar as possible to the earlier part. Some alterations have, however, become necessary particularly in order to make use of word processing equipment in Lancaster and Cardiff.

Archives relating to excavations published here

will be deposited in the Lancashire Record Office, Bow Lane, Preston. These will normally consist of site notes, the originals or copies of all plans and sections made, the originals of the figures illustrated in this volume, background correspndence and records along with the photographic record of the excavations. It and other Ribchester material may be consulted by reference to the County Archaeologist at the Record Office. In addition the Cumbria and Lancashire Unit (University of Lancaster) hold copies of most of the material relating to excavations with which it has been concerned. For reasons outlined in part 1, finds relating to the present excavations will be temporarily stored by the Unit but it is hoped eventually to deposit all finds in the Ribchester Museum.

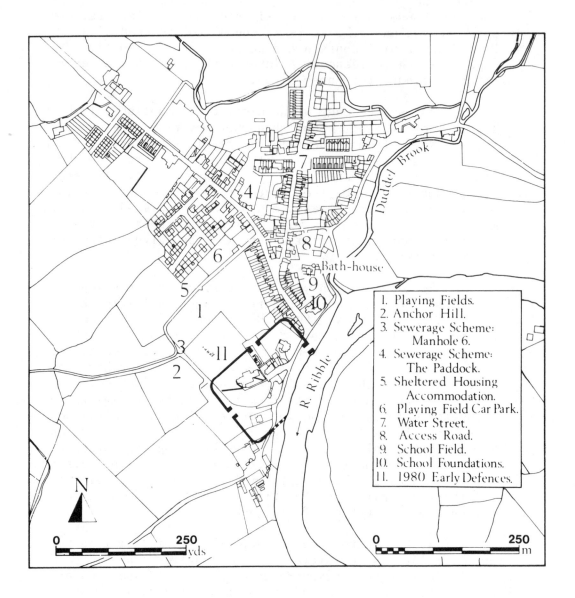

1. Playing Fields.
2. Anchor Hill.
3. Sewerage Scheme: Manhole 6.
4. Sewerage Scheme: The Paddock.
5. Sheltered Housing Accommodation.
6. Playing Field Car Park.
7. Water Street.
8. Access Road.
9. School Field.
10. School Foundations.
11. 1980 Early Defences.

Fig.1. Location map of sites within the civil settlement.

Chapter 1.

INTRODUCTION

As already stated, this part of the **Ribchester Excavations** series attempts to gather together reports on all the major excavations undertaken beteeen 1968 and 1980 within the civil settlement around the Roman fort at Ribchester, with the single exception of the re-examination of the Bath-house which we hope it may prove possible to include in a later part. A number of small scale excavations and watching briefs have also been excluded as well as excavations conducted prior to 1968. These and other sites will receive mention in summary form in the gazetteer which is also planned.

Most of the excavations detailed here have been undertaken as the result of development threats and it is perhaps not surprising, therefore, that they are concentrated upon the north and east sides of the Roman fort. River action has, of course, removed much of the south side of the fort and, with it, any associated civil settlement, but we are conscious that a more balanced view of the civilian settlement will only be available when the west side of the fort can be sampled more adequately.

The sites excavated do allow us to say something of the chronology of the northern and eastern civil settlement at Ribchester. Virtually all sites investigated produced plentiful finds of the late first and second centuries A.D. and it was certainly this period which saw the zenith of settlement in the areas investigated. By the mid third century the civilian area seems to have shrunk considerably. Of sites reported upon here, the Access Road produced a very small amount of third and fourth century pottery, but only the School Field and Anchor Hill (sites 9 and 2 on fig.1, p.8) yielded much in the way of later finds. On all sites, finds of the latest fort phase (equivalemt to Hadrian's Wall Period IV) are conspicuous by almost total their absence.

This outline chronology can be used to help us begin the task of examining the geographical development of the settlement. Excavations in the Playing Fields and the Sheltered Housing site (Fig.1, sites 1 and 5) show that the settlement to the north of the fort grew rapidly in the period between the foundation of the fort (assumed to be c.A.D.80) and the early second century. Sites to the east and north-east of the fort seem to show the same pattern, while the plentiful first and second century pottery from the Water Street site (fig.1, site 7 ; not reported upon here, but the finds were kindly made available by the excavator, Mr J.Ridge) show that the settlement had spread considerably in a north-easterly direction within this period.

The axes of the early settlement are likely to have been the roads leading from the north and east gates of the fort. That from the north gate runs across the present Playing Fields and Playing Fields Car Park towards a junction with the present

Ribchester-Longridge road (just beyond the north-east limits of our fig.1, p.8). West of this road lie the Playing Fields and Sheltered Housing sites (fig.1, sites 1 and 5) which between them suggest an area of intense settlement served by a network of branch roads, some of which were of a very substantial nature. The Sheltered Housing site (Chapter 5) also yielded a ditch which could be part of the defences of the civil settlement of a similar type to that found at Melandra (Webster 1973,p.59) and elsewhere (see this volume Chapter 9). The layout east of the road from the north gate is less clear as only the Playing Field Car Park and Sewerage Scheme excavations (Chapters 5 and 3) have sampled the area and both seem likely to have traversed only the northern fringe of the settlement.

The second major axis of the settlement is likely to have been the road which ran from the east gate of the fort northwards towards the bath house and perhaps towards a road heading North from the Ribble crossing (always assumed to be East of Ribchester itself, cf. Margary 1967, Route 7c, p.377 ff.). Whether there was a more direct route East to the Ribble crossing is hard to tell but it is probable that the Duddel Brook formed a barrier to communications in the Roman period as it does today and it is probably worth bearing in mind that the present route to the Ribble Bridge runs north from the village, before striking East. If this pattern is similar to that of the Roman period, it would explain the considerable spread of the civil settlement to the north of the east gate of the fort (at least as far as the Water Street site, fig.1, no.7). The bath house and the remains in the School Field (ibid. site 9) suggest major structures just north-east of the fort. It is also worth bearing in mind that, although the exact findspots of RIB 587 and 588 are not known, this was on the river bank suggesting a location just east of the fort for the temple or temples they indicate.

As already stated, the late vicus was apparently much smaller than its predecessor. To the north and north-east of the fort, settlement seems to have ceased by the mid third century at the latest. The Baths also seem to have ceased operation by this time (cf. Godwin 1979). The School Field, however, produces a wide range of third century pieces including much fineware (cf. Part 3, Chap.2, section g) and there is every indication of a major building in the vicinity in the third and perhaps into the fourth century. The School Field is, however, within one hundred metres of the fort and the late settlement would have been small indeed if compressed within the narrow space available between the fort and the Duddel Brook on the east side of the fort. It is certainly not unknown for the major focus of a civil settlement to 'migrate' around the perimeter of a fort (see, for instance, the settlement at Brough-under-Stainmore, Jones 1977, p.39). It is just possible that this happenned at Ribchester and that later civilian occupation centred on the west and east gates rather than the North and East gates as previously (the south gate is inherently improbable as a focus because of its assumed proximity to the River. The anomolous collection of pottery from Anchor Hill, north-west of the fort (pottery nos. 183-189) may be an indicator that this is so. This collection contains more fourth century pottery than the other civil sites and some of the few pieces which could be mid-late fourth century. The work at Anchor Hill was, however, small scale and inconclusive as regards structures while the sewer trench observed in 1976 in this area (see chapter 3) yielded no late pieces. The blocking of the west gate in the late period (see below) also argues against a large late western settlement. It would thus be rash to draw any conclusions from this one site but it does serve to indicate the importance of further investigations to the west and north-west of the fort when opportunity arises.

It is worth noting that the radical changes in the size or location of the civil settlement appear to coincide approximately with changes in the fort interior. The 1970 excavations in the **retentura** showed that at least two barrack buildings were demolished and not rebuilt some time in the first half of the third century (Edwards & Webster 1985, p.37). If this represents an actual reduction in the size of the garrison, and there seems to be no reason to suppose that it does not, then the coincidence with the apparent reduction in the size of the vicus becomes significant. Could it be that the garrison of Ribchester in the later third century was much reduced and that it is this which had such a dramatic effect on the size of the dependent civil settlement?

One other detail of the 1970 excavations within the fort may be noted. Apparently in the late third century, the west gate of the fort was blocked and the structure partially demolished (Edwards & Webster 1985, 26-7). This event should have had some effect upon the civil settlement on the west of the fort. If this was not already reduced in size, one would expect the blocking of the link with the fort interior to have caused the settlement on the west to dwindle rapidly. If this were indeed so then the anomalous nature of the Anchor Hill pottery is again emphasised and once again the plea must be for excavation to the west of the fort.

If we view the excavations reported upon in this part in social and economic terms we can see considerable variation between the various areas investigated. The streets beneath the Playing Field (see Figs.2-3) were probably originally lined with wooden framed strip houses, a type usually associated with shops and workshops. Particularly in the later second century, the area was apparently given over to small scale industrial activity associated with hearths (see pp.26-7). In passing, it may be noted that the Water Street excavations (Fig.1, site 7) also yielded evidence of 'industrial' activity in the form of two crucibles and a crucible cover (to be reported upon in a later part in this series) and a pottery waster indicative of a kiln nearby.

An indication of commercial activity elsewhere in the

settlement may be the large number of Dressel 20 South Spanish oil
amphorae recovered from parts of the Sewerage Scheme (Chapter 3)
and from the Access Road site (Chapter 6). These and other sites
also yielded a few wine amphorae from South Gaul (Dressel 30/
Pelichet 47) and from Italy (Dressel 2-4) but it is clear that the
Ribchester settlement will have been more notable for its oil shops
than for its wine bars.

By contrast, the area around the bath house yielded a large
quantity of fine pottery. This may be partly for chronological
reasons - the sites survived into the period when colour coated
finewares were plentiful - but all the sites in the area (the
Access Road, the School Field, the School foundations) are notable
for either the quantity or the quality of their samian ware (see
part 3, nos. 60-145). Despite the shops postulated north of the
baths (Chapter 6) this wealth of fine pottery may imply occupation
of a more residential type. As will be seen, the trial work in the
School Field suggests a major building in the vicinity and this
could be the area where the **mansio** should be sought.

In summary, therefore, the excavations reported upon here
which, it must be remembered, sample only the north and east vicus,
suggest a settlement booming in the late first and second century
but contracting rapidly in the third, apparently at the same time
as changes within the fort itself. By the mid fourth century, the
settlement outside the fort was virtually non-existent. As already
hinted, this pattern may well reflect the intensity of military
activity within the fort. Certainly, on the basis of very limited
excavation within the residential quarters of the fort, it would
seem that the first and second centuries saw the fort most fully
occupied, while the third saw a contraction of the garrison.
Although Ribchester is not without inscriptions of the mid third
century, the great majority of the building records date from the
first quarter of that century and earlier (cf. Grace Simpson in
Edwards & Webster 1985, Chapter 1 and RIB nos.583-595). The coin
list from the fort itself, also shows anomalies which may indicate
a lack of activity in the second half of the third century
(Shotter, ibid. Chapter 8).

Whatever the explanation for the reduction in settlement
size during the third century, the total absence of any civilian
settlement in the later fourth century in the areas investigated
requires some different explanation. Both the coins and the
pottery show that the fort was occupied during the last half (and
probably well into the last quarter) of the fourth century (Edwards
& Webster 1985, pp.81-3, 87) but with the exception of a few pieces
nothing which is diagnostically late fourth century has been
recovered from excavations in the civil settlement. If the late
fort, like other late establishments, resembled more a fortified
military town than it did the earlier fort then the absence of
remains outside is explicable. The ultimate fate of the Roman
civil settlement at Ribchester may have been to be absorbed into the
fort itself.

Chapter 2.
TRIAL EXCAVATIONS IN THE PLAYING FIELDS, 1968–9.
By B.J.N.Edwards, G.D.B.Jones & P.V.Webster.

With the kind permission of the Playing Fields Committee, excavations were undertaken in September 1968 and May–June 1969 in the western part of the Playing Fields. Work was under the auspices of the Ribble Archaeological Society and with support of the Carnegie Trust. We are most grateful to Society members for their considerable help.

The area examined lay north of the northern defences of the Roman Fort and west of the line of the road which was assumed to run northwards from the north gate of the Fort (see Fig.1 site 1). The area thus seemed likely to contain parts of the civil settlement or perhaps some extra-mural military structure. The area available was extensive and it was in an attempt to select from this areas suitable for excavation by hand that four cuts were made mechanically (see plan, fig 2). In the event, the information revealed by these slots was so complex that work outside them was not possible with the limited resources of time and money available

Of the four slots cut, trenches 1 and 4 ran approximately parallel to the churchyard wall (and thus to the northern defences of the fort) and about 6 feet from the wall. Trench 2 was approximately parallel to trench 1 but c.55 feet from the wall, while trench 3 ran approximately at right angles to the other trenches and the churchyard wall. The slots were cut by machine and their interpretation is thus chiefly dependent upon their sections together with such plans as could be recovered by control of the base to which the machine operated and by limited excavation by hand. Four sections were drawn (indicated on Fig.2) of which three are illustrated in Fig.3-6. To avoid unduly cumbersome figures, the drawn sections have been divided but a continuous scale is used. Plans, where shown, use the same portion of the continuous scale as their corresponding sections. Where necessary, plans also show depths from the surface in feet and inches (as used for the initial measurements). The originals of all four section drawings will be deposited in the site archive. Trench and level details in the text below are everywhere given in arabic numerals separated by a 'decimal' point: thus 1.10 = trench 1, layer 10.

The excavations suggest activity almost entirely within the first two centuries A.D and divisable into four phases, as set out below.

I.Primary Activity

The natural subsoil on the site, as elsewhere at Ribchester, is a sandy water-washed gravel (2.15, 2.24). Parts of trench 1 skimmed this natural subsoil but it was cut (and clearly defined) only in trench 2. Here, two features indicate slight

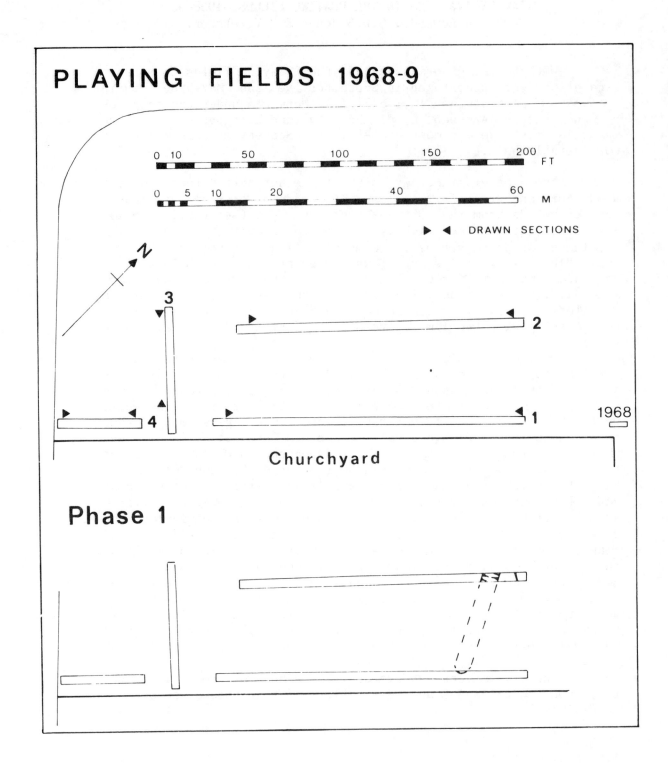

Fig.2.

activity prior to the main construction phase. A construction slot (2.73), presumably part of a timber building, lay at the east end of trench 2, while about 9 feet (2.7m) to the west was a V-shaped ditch measuring 5 feet (1.5m) from the eastern lip to the centre point. It was about 4 feet (1.2m) deep, apparently with a small clearance gulley at the base. The latter contained a small amount of silt (2.71) and about 18 inches of further silting (2.70). This latter had a high organic content. The butt end of what may be the same ditch was found at the eastern end of trench 1 (centred on the 130ft mark on the drawn section, fig.5, see also fig.2). No other features were located which are certainly primary but this may well be due to the fact (already stated) that the natural subsoil was not defined in all parts of the excavation. The pit, 2.16a, although cut into the subsoil (fig.6) contains material which suggests that it belongs to a later phase.

There is no direct dating evidence for Phase 1. However, the overlying Phase 2 structures seem likely to have been constructed in the later first or very early second century. Primary activity in the Flavian period thus seems possible. Despite the failure to locate any surviving remains of a rampart backing the ditch, this nevertheless has the character of a military defensive work and the earliest activity on the site may thus be associated with a defensive system connected with the initial Flavian fort at Ribchester. Perhaps the defences are those of an annexe to the first fort or even that of a compound used by the fort builders. One wonders how the ditch relates to that revealed by the 1980 excavations in the churchyard (cf.Olivier in Edwards & Webster 1985, pp.6 & 47; also Wilson 1984 on defensive outworks generally). It appears to be too early to relate to that on the Sheltered Housing site (see Chapter 4 below).

II. Early timber buildings.

The main occupation of the area sampled started in Phase 2. A succession of timber buildings with intervening alleyways, probably of the late 1st/early 2nd centuries, ran north-south across the southern part of the site. Prior to the contruction of the Phase 2 buildings, levelling appears to have taken place over the whole area sampled by trench 1. Occupation material (1.8,8b,8c) was dumped to form the base for subsequent building.

Building 1 was represented by a destruction level of charcoal lying directly on the make-up level, 1.8 (charcoal 1.11 at datum 139-149 feet). Above Building 1 a layer of gravelly make-up (1.12, 1.9) separated it from the clay floor of the succeeding **Building** 2 (1.13, 6c, 6a) cut by later building activity (Buildings 8-9 see below). The possible slot 1.7 may belong with Building 1, while the gravel 1.18 may represent an alleyway to the west.

The occupation and mixed occupation/destruction material 1.26 and 1.33 suggest the site of a further building edged by slots at either end (datum points 115 feet and 130 feet) but the clay

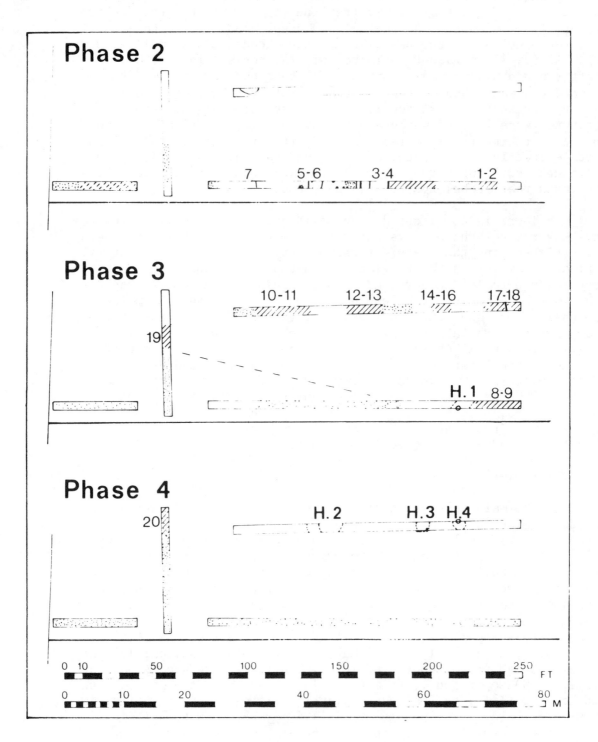

Fig.3.

floors and distinct destruction deposits which generally distinguish the phase 2 structures elsewhere are missing.

To the west of Buildings 1-2, two successive pairs of timber buildings (3-4 and 5-6) survived beneath a later road surface which had sealed them so completely that in places they had scarcely rotted since the time of their abandonment. Buildings 3-6 provide many indications as to the type of timber construction employed in this area of the civil settlement at Ribchester. Upright timbers were generally about 4in x 2in (10 x 5 cms) sharpened at one end and either hammered directly into the ground or into prepared holes which were then refilled, sometimes with stone chocks. One timber found out of context measured 9in (23cms) square and indicates that timber sizes were not totally standard. Internal partition walls were of wattle, perhaps without daub coating, if the wall base 1.102 and the collapsed wattle fragment in Building 6 are typical. Exterior walls were of wattle and daub between timber uprights. It seems likely that in most cases the wattle and daub was pulled off the wooden framework and burnt on demolition. Floors were probably generally of clay or straw (a compacted mass of the latter material, 1.101, was found in Building 3). Boarded floors are also a possibility (cf. Building 4).

The wooden buildings had been demolished to ground level. Some indication of the methods used to secure members within the superstructure did, however, survive. A well preserved tenon (now in Ribchester Museum, a photograph is in the site archive) indicates the type of jointing used and shows that the tenon was formed with the aid of a saw. The size of hole in the tenon itself suggests that it was pegged in place. The finding of simple iron clamps indicates a further method of securing joints.

The relatively slight nature of the timber used in Buildings 3-6, together with the method of bedding them into the ground, makes it unlikely that the buildings were ever more than one storey high, for not only would the timbers be too small for greater height but the sheer weight of a taller structure would have been likely to press the sharpened stakes further and further into the relatively soft soil in which they were bedded. Few roof tiles were found on the excavation and so some other type of roofing (i.e. thatch or wooden shingles) may be implied.

The exact limits of **Building 3** are hard to define. A post surviving within a stone-chocked post-hole at datum point 59-60 feet probably represents the western limit, although the post at datum point 67 ft. (see plan fig.5) and the edge of floor 1.101 could also indicate a possible line for the external wall. At the eastern end of the building, the clay floor 1,35 may belong to Building 3 with the outer eastern wall represented by the slot at datum point 103 ft. Alternatively 1.35 may represent an entirely different building, although this seems less likely in the absence of any indication of substantial walling between 1.101 and 1.35. As revealed by the section, the internal arrangements of Building 3 show seven probable wall lines at datum points 59/60ft.,70ft.,

73/4ft., 80/81ft., 83ft., 91ft. and 103ft. and it seems likely that alterations in the internal layout of the building may have taken place during its use. Central to the building was the floor 1.101, a lightly gravelled surface laid directly on the levelling layer 1.8 with compacted straw above. Of particular interest was the base of a wattle wall (1.102 at datum 80ft.). This may be one of the alterations to Building 3 already suggested, as it appeared to have been inserted into the straw flooring and did not reach the base of 1.101. The wattle consisted of two vertical round poles about 3 inches (7.5cms) in diameter, placed about 2 feet (0.6m) apart with wattle woven around them. The panel had been broken off at floor level and no daub survived on the extant portion. In this connection, the wattle panel from Building 6 (see below) may be noted. This too lacked daub and it could be that both panels are representative of the internal divisions of the building. The excavated portion of the wall in Building 3 clearly belonged to a panel placed intermediate between the major wooden uprights of the frame. The floor 1.101 yielded leather fragments.

Building 3 was demolished down to its floor level. The timber uprights seem to have been sawn off at this level and even the wattle panel 1.102 was not removed below floor level. No extensive destruction deposit survived, although debris from the building was almost certainly incorporated in the levelling for the next structure (i.e. in 1.97 and 1.36).

Building 3 was replaced by **Building 4** in approximately the same position. Again, the exact limits of the building are difficult to define but the western side could well be the slot at datum 61 ft. with one room represented by the clay floor 1.96 and another by the clay floor 1.40. A surviving post and wall line marked the western edge of the latter (datum 77 ft.). Floor 1.40 was overlain by destruction debris (1.41-2); this included charred timber and it may be that the floor had once been planked.

Building 5 would appear to have been contemporary with Building 3. One wall was marked by the slot 1.99 (see fig.4, plan, datum 46-8 ft.). To the east a spread of gravel and stone may represent an alleyway between Buildings 5 and 3. Only a small portion of the interior of Building 5 was excavated. Also probably contemporary with Building 3 was the successor to Building 5, **Building** 6. The east wall of this structure was represented by a surviving stake at datum 54 ft. The internal floor was the light gravel spread which formed the upper part of layer 1.95. There appears to have been a gap of about 5 feet between Buildings 6 and 3 but no metalled alleyway. Lying across the floor surface of Building 6 (1.95) was the remains of a panel of wattlework (see **Britannia** 1 [1970] pl.XXXII,A and our fig.4, plan, datum 42-4 ft.). The fragment was in an excellent state of preservation and measured about 2 feet (0.6m) square. The vertical members were about 1 ft (0.3m) apart and less sturdy than those used in wall 1.102 in Building 3. The wattlework was presumably derived from some other part of Building 6, perhaps the wall marked by the stake holes at datum 46 ft. which were placed at approximately the right intervals

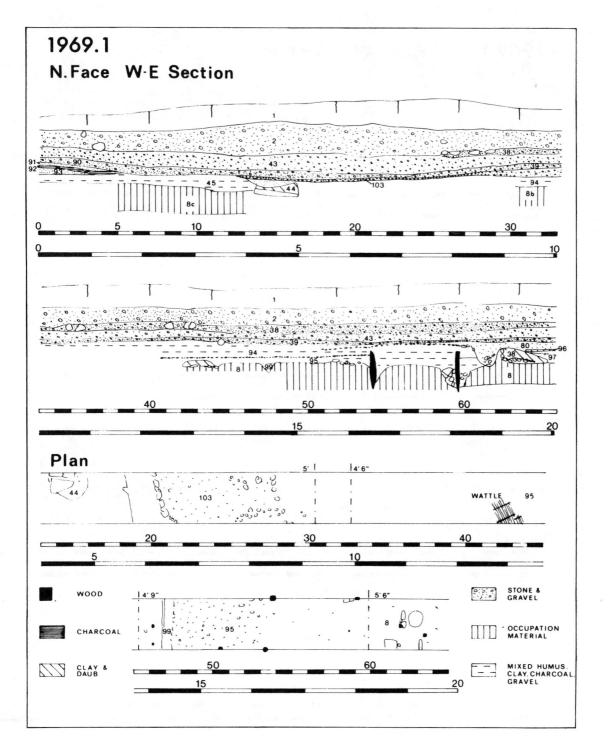

Fig.4.

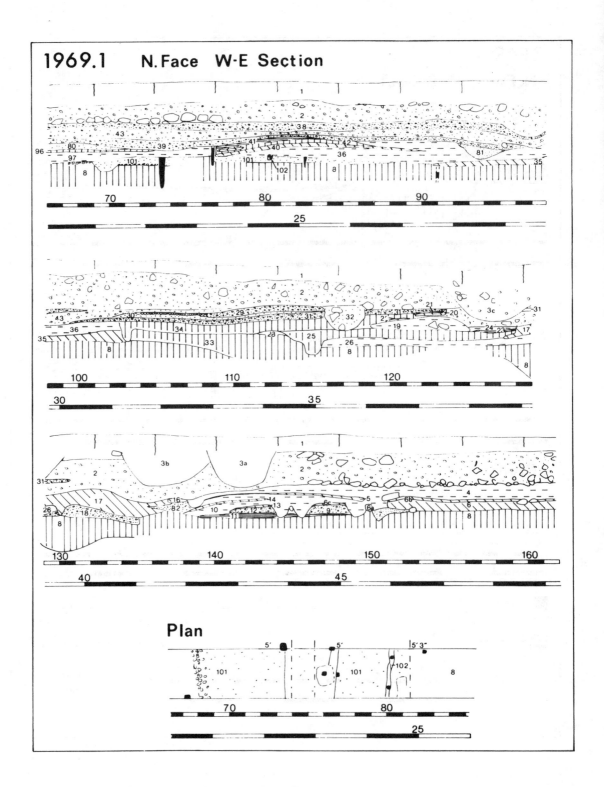

Fig.5.

to accomodate the vertical members of the surviving piece. The wattle lacked any sign of daub and may be presumed, therefore, to have formed part of an internal dividing wall. The wattle was lifted and treated by the North-West Museums and Art Gallery Service and is now housed in the Ribchester Museum.

There were no certain signs of a building later than Building 6 which might have been contemporary with Building 4. A spread of gravel ran west from the presumed west wall of Building 4 and partially sealed Building 6 (datum 50-60 ft.). This suggests that during the lifetime of Building 4, Building 6 was demolishefd and partially replaced by an open metalled area.

Phase 2 building levels were not fully investigated in the most westerly 40 feet of trench 1. However, Building 5 can be assumed to have continued into this area and probably abutted the building which yielded the collapsed daub 1.44 (datum 13-16 ft.) and the possible wall line (fig.4, plan, datum 21 ft.). This structure, called here **Building 7**, presumably marks the site of a building contemporary with Buildings 3 and 5-6. It was overlain by the gravel spread 1.103 which may itself be an extension of the gravelled area West of Building 4. Perhaps also contemporary with Building 4 is the levelling 1.45 and the earliest period of the road 1.93 at the extreme west end of trench 1. A similar pattern was observable in trench 3 (see fig.7). Here 3.7 is equivalent to the initial levelling layer 1.8 and layers 3.22, 3.4-5 and 3.10 are all probably contemporary with 1.45. The lowest road, perhaps equivalent to 1.93 is 3.6. Phase 2 was represented in trench 4 by layers which included occupation and destruction material (4.3, 4.5, 4.7 and 4.15) but which lacked any clear indication of buildings. A strip of sand and gravel 12 feet (3.66m) wide at the extreme western end of the trench (4.6) may represent a further roadway.

Perhaps contemporary with the later part of phase 2 was the large pit 2.16a. Also certainly pre-dating Phase 3, although not necessarily by very much, was the levelling 2.14 and 2.16, This levelling may well contain occupation and destruction material from the phase 2 buildings further south, spread across the area to the north of the Phase 2 occupation in order to facilitate new development (i.e. Phase 3 building).

The outline chronology of Phase 2 is clear. Levelling prior to development contained mainly first century material but the occupation material from the buildings themselves probably falls within the early part of the second century. The levelling (1.8) included Flavian samian (no.1, c.A.D.70-85) from beneath the floor of Building 3 and Flavian-Trajanic samian (no.2) from below Building 5. The floor of Building 3 contained a coin of Domitian (no.674) and pottery which appears to be predominantly Trajanic but perhaps runs into the Hadrianic period (coarse pottery nos.154-157). The collapse of Building 7 (1.44) yielded material including a samian form 37 base in the orange micaceous fabric typical of Lezoux production prior to c.A.D.120 and also a vessel

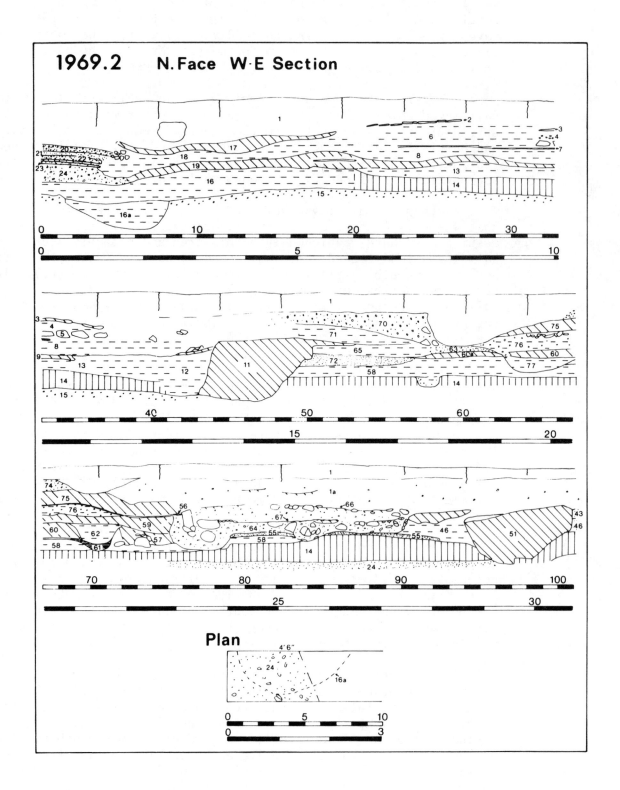

Fig.6.

of form 18/31 of Les Martres origin. One certainly Central Gaulish scrap from the levelling 1.8 could be intrusive but is not necessarily incompatible with a Trajanic/ early Hadrianic date for Buildings 1, 3, 5, 6 and 7. The later buildings (2 and 4) and contemporary levels are approximately dated by a Central Gaulish beaker fragment probably from the wall trench of Building 4 and by contemporary material from trenches 3 and 4 (pottery archive) but more particularly by implication from the better dated levels which bracket them stratigraphically.

The pit 2.16a and the levelling 2.16 and 2.14 all seem to include material which is slightly later than the latest material from the Phase 2 buildings further South. Thus, while Flavian and Trajanic pottery is present (e.g. nos. 156, 162) so is Hadrianic/ early Antonine (nos. 5-6, 159) and it is to the latter period that the levelling must be ascribed. This is also presumably the period which saw the end of the Phase 2 occupation of Buildings 2 and 4 and the beginning of the Phase 3 remodelling of the civil settlement in this area.

III. Later timber buildings.

Phase 3 saw a totally new layout in this part of the Civil Settlement, probably based upon a road which traversed the central part of trench 1 completely sealing the levelled remains of Buildings 3-7. Three principal layers of surfacing were apparent in trench 1 (1.90/39, 1.43, 1.38). It seems likely that this road cut across trench 1 at a shallow diagonal in a line approximately ENE to WSW and that the same road is represented in trench 3 by layers 3.17, 3.9 and 3.12 and possibly in trench 4 by 4.13-14 although this would give an unusually large width to the road and the thinner road levels in trench 4 may be part of a side road (see plan fig.3).

To the east of the new road, occupation continued over the site of Buildings 1-2. Here **Building 8** is represented only by a short length of clay floor (1.14, datum 138-143 ft) with possible post holes immediately to the east. The succeeding structure, **Building 9**, was evidenced by much more substantial remains with clay floors 1.5 and 1.6/6b extending over 23 feet (7m) from datum 139 ft onwards.

Perhaps contemporary with Building 9 was **Hearth 1.** This was of bowl type, formed by dumping clay (1.17) into a previously excavated hole and then hollowing out the bowl from the centre of this mass. The bowl survived on the South side of the trench (i.e. the side away from the drawn section) and was filled with layers of ash. Lying between the junction of the ashy fill and the clay lining was a sestertius of Trajan (see Part 3, Chapter 3, no.676). This had been unaffected by the heat of the hearth and so had presumably been deposited, with the ashy fill which sealed it, after the hearth went out of use. The fill certainly appeared to be

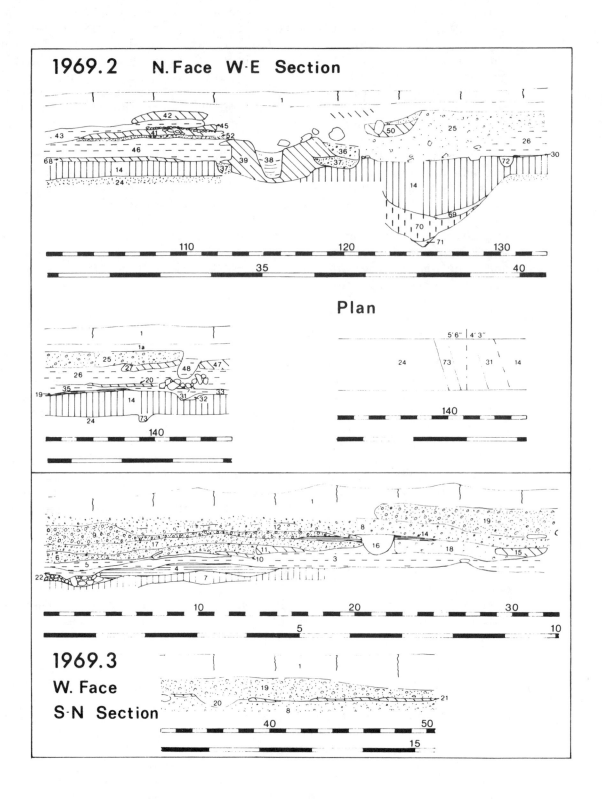

Fig. 7.

'industrial waste' and other hearths in the vicinity may be implied.

Buildings 10-17 all lay east of the supposed line of the Phase 3 road and east of what may be a side road (2.20-24). Buildings 10-11 were immediately east of this road. **Building 10** was contemporary with the road surface 2.24 and was represented by a clay floor (2.9, 2.19) extending a minimum of about 29 feet (8.8m) along the section and possibly further (to datum 44ft, a total of 38 ft or 11.6m). No definite wall positions were evident but the daub patches and charcoal lens at datum 17-20ft may represent a demolished wall. The mere length of Building 10 floor sectioned suggests that the building may have been cut longitudinally and it may well have fronted onto the roadway 2.23/24. The succeeding structure, **Building 11** was much more fragmentary but may well, originally, have been as extensive as its predecessor. A clay floor, 2.17 extends east of the roadway 2.20-22. It is interupted (at about datum 19ft.) but appears to be continued from about datum 20ft. as a layer of stone slabs (2.2). East of datum 27ft. this is again disturbed by recent activity but it seems likely that the heavy stone and gravel, 2.4-5 and possible daub, 2.3 may mark a continuation of the building (see fig.6).

The area east of Building 10 may well have remained open for the earlier part of Phase 3, as it contained a slot (at datum 57-8ft.) overlain by further occupation debris and a pit (2.77). Over this lay the remains of **Building 12** represented by the clay floor 2.60a, 2.60 and perhaps 2.57. The pit 2.62 (datum 70ft.) may have been structural and the mass of clay and burnt material 2.59 probably represents the demolition debris from a wall. A fragment of the succeeding building (**Building 13**) remained as the clay floor 2.75. The large pit with heavy stone fill at datum 76-79ft. (see fig.6) may be a large post-pit and could also belong with Building 13. Less certain is the relationship of the surfaces 2.55, 2.67 and 2.66 to Buildings 12-13. Of these, the sandy level 2.55 may be an alleyway associated with Building 12, or even a floor associated with it. Surface 2.67 seems to be stratigraphically linked with the large pit at datum 76-9 ft already mentioned. and may, therefore, be linked with Building 13. Both 2.67 and 2.66 could be lightly metalled alleyways or yards or even internal floors.

At the eastern end of trench 2, Phase 3 building levels had been partially destroyed by Phase 4 structures. However, a succession of clay floors seem evident between datum 101ft. and 112ft. and presumably represent the remains of three buildings, the lower clay floor (2.68 see fig.7) being **Building 14**, the intermediate gravel (2.52), clay (2.41) and its overlying cobble surface, **Building 15** and the short length of clay floor above (2.42), **Building 16.**

Apparently positioned between the roadway clipped by the west end of trench 2 and that which runs across the southern half of trench 3 was a further building. This, **Building 19**, appears to have been contemporary with road surface 3.17, but was evidenced only by slight traces, the charcoal destruction deposit 3.14 and the clay and gravel floor fragment 3.15 (fig.7). The pit or slot 3.16 may be part of a later adaptation of the same structure.

As already stated, the material from the levelling prior to Phase 3 (in trench 2) includes sherds of Hadrianic to early Antonine date (Part 3, pottery nos.6 & 161-4) and this provides the most likely starting date for the earliest Phase 3 buildings (Buildings 8, 10, 12, 14 and 17). Later building activity within Phase 3 is to be dated to the Antonine period and probably to after c.A.D.150 as the levelling below Building 11 (2.8 and 2.18), probably in part derived from the destruction of Building 10, included samian (no.10) dated c.A.D.150-180, while level 2.64, which was perhaps contemporary with Building 13, included material of similar date (no.11). Hadrianic to mid-Antonine coarse pottery came from above the slightly later surface 2.67. In general, an early to mid Antonine date would suit the evidence from Phase 3.

IV. The latest buildings and the industrial phase.

In the southern part of the area sampled, Phase 4 was marked by the dumping of vast quantities of stone and gravel over the entire area traversed by trench 1 and the 1968 trial slot (see plan, fig.2). This dump was at least 2 feet (0.6m) deep at the eastern end of trench 1 (1.2) but thinned to 1 foot (0.3m) where it ran over the Phase 3 road. It is probably represented by 3.8 in trench 3 and by 4.2. It was overlain by further dumping at the northern end of trench 3 (3.19) but appears to be entirely absent in trench 2. The massive operation represented by this stone and gravel dump is difficult to explain. The combined evidence of trenches 1 and 3 suggest that a large width of land was treated in this way and we seem to be dealing with more than simply a resurfacing of the roadway. It may be noted that the area sampled immediately to the South in 1980 (Edwards & Webster 1985, p.47 & p.6, fig.1) suggested a wide open area north of the stone fort defences. Perhaps we are seeing here an extension of this open defensive zone.

It would seem that the northern edge of the Phase 4 dump served as a base for **Building 20** as clay and daub lay upon the surface of 3.8 at its northern end (3.21). A possible pit (3.20) associated with this building was sectioned at datum 35-38 ft. Building 20 appears to have been demolished to make way for a secondary phase of dumping (3.19).
Also ascribed to Phase 4 are the three hearths (2-4) located in trench 2. All are of similar contruction to hearth 1 (see above), that is a hole filled with clay, with a bowl hollowed out within the clay. In all cases burning within the hearth had not been so intense as to harden all the clay block but only the clay immediately adjacent to the bowl itself.

It seems likely that **Hearth 1** (2.11 see fig.3 & fig.6) was aligned approximately east-west and that the area to its west which contained much charcoal (2.12) is part of the 'praefurnium'. The alignment of **Hearth** 3 (2.51, see Figs.3 & 6) is not certain, but of interest is the revetment found on its south side. This seems most likely to represent a temporary shoring of the hole dug for the hearth prior to the deposition of the clay. The central bowl of **Hearth 4** survived (2.38-9, figs.3 & 7) approximately 1.5 feet (0.45m) deep and resembling an inverted and truncated cone. It was filled to a depth of about one foot (0.3m) with waste material which included some domestic rubbish (including a samian vessel of Curle form 11 dated to the Hadrianic-Antonine period).

No slags were found in definite relationship to any of the hearths sectioned. Similar furnaces at Wilderspool have been associated with iron smelting (Thompson 1965, pp.73-6). The low temperatures evidently reached in all the hearths at Ribchester indicate, however, that they were not used for smelting and this is confirmed by the absence of smelting slag on the site. Such slag as there was from the 1969 excavation would be consistent with the smithing of iron and this may have been the function of the hearths located. No structures definitely associated with hearths 2-4 were located.

With the exception of the samian fragments from Hearth 4, already mentioned, there was litte dating evidence from Phase 4 levels. However, it is worth noting that there was very little pottery from the excavation, even from unstratified material, which need be later than c.A.D.200 and, indeed, little that is even likely to be third century or later. In view of the dating for Phase 3, it seems safe, therefore, to suggest a mid to late Antonine date for Phase 4.

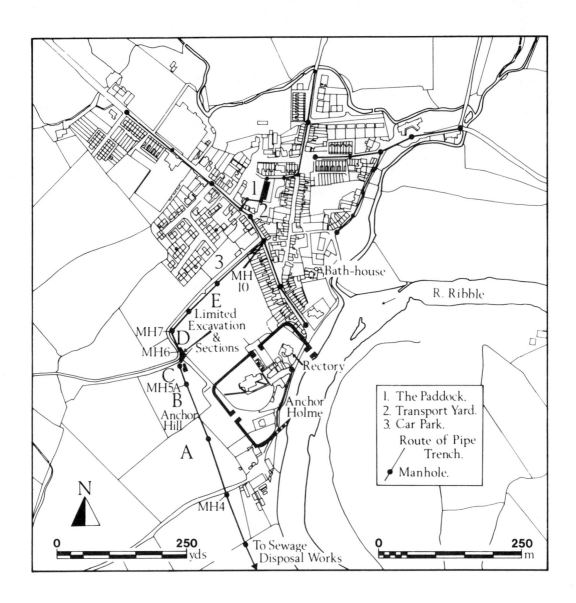

Fig.8. Sewerage Scheme. General Map.

Chapter 3.
EMERGENCY EXCAVATIONS AND WATCHING BRIEF CONDUCTED DURING THE CONSTRUCTION OF THE NEW SEWERAGE SCHEME.
By A.C.H.Olivier.

Introduction.

In 1976, work was begun on a new sewerage scheme. Excavations in 1969 (Chapter 2 above) had already established the archaeological potential of much of the area involved in this work, and by the early summer of 1976, it was apparent that fairly large scale disturbance of archaeological deposits was taking place. Consequently, the recently appointed Field Officer for Lancashire was asked to conduct a full time watching brief during the excavation of the pipe trench.

Work was initiated between the new sewage works by the bank of the River Ribble (SD 651 344) and the junction of the car park access road with Church Street (SD 6500 3525). The trench was dug by a mechanical excavator to a width of 2-3 m. and a depth of c.4 m. and only a short length was open at any one time. Observation was, therefore, extremely difficult.

In the area of Manhole 6, however, it was possible both to record the sections, and to undertake some limited excavation. This area lay to the north-west of the fort, adjacent to the churchyard wall (fig.8), close to the western end of trenches I and IV excavated in 1969 (see Chapter 2 above), and was, therefore, known to contain a portion, at least, of the civil settlement associated with the fort. Only the sides of the pipe trench could be recorded in detail, and none of the main sections was located according to archaeological considerations. The excavated areas were small and fragmented, and although this work did aid in the interpretation of the sections, no comprehensive plan could be recovered. Excavation of a larger area was initiated slightly closer to the fort. However, extreme weather conditions during the drought of 1976 precluded the confident identification of structures or other major features in the very dry clay subsoil, and work here was abandoned after a short period in order to open a more important and promising area.

A small plot of completely undeveloped waste land known locally as the "Paddock", lying immediately south of the Black Bull car park (SD 6501 3544) was made available for a period of three weeks in advance of pipe laying operations. The Paddock lies in close proximity to the site of the "Transport Yard" (SD 6501 3530) where in 1967, the Rev. G.E. Stevens discovered six cremation burials in amphorae, enclosed in cists. An area of c.22.0 x 8.0 m. was stripped of topsoil and several trenches were dug by machine. No burials of any description were encountered, however, although traces of other activity were revealed.

Observation and recording during pipelaying along the streets was more difficult than elsewhere. The continued use of the village streets by traffic at all times during the sewerage work restricted the maximum width of the pipe trench to c.1.5 m. This narrow trench was shored and consequently it was only possible to observe the presence of archaeological material, and not to record any sections.

Part A describes the results of the more detailed work conducted in the areas of Manhole 6 and the Paddock. Part B is a report of the general watching brief carried out during the excavation of the pipe trench and the laying of the pipeline. Much of the material resulting from this watching brief was unassociated, unstratified, and, of necessity, inadequately recorded. The considerable size of the Archive is, therefore, out of proportion with the value of the results achieved and it is only appropriate to publish here a summary of the main results.

All finds are to be deposited in Ribchester Museum. The original archive will be deposited at the Lancashire Record Office; one copy is retained at the Cumbria and Lancashire Archaeology Unit, University of Lancaster, and microfiche copies will be deposited at the National Monuments Record and Ribchester Museum.

Summary of Archive Contents

A. (1) Published Report
   (2) The full report from which the published report has been abstracted. It includes the detailed description of all excavated features together with the analysis and listing of all classified and bulk finds. In addition it includes the full consolidated field records, defining structural and stratigraphical relations, annoted with chronological data, and an index to all finds.

B. Site Records
   (1) Field note books containing the description of all features.
   (2) Site indices: Soil samples, Selected finds, Bulk Finds codes, Sections.
   (3) Surveying notes.

C. Drawings and sections
   (1) Index to plans and original plan drawings.
   (2) Index to sections and original section drawings.
   (3) Original field drawings (objects)

D. Photographs
   (1) Index to monochrome photographs; negatives and contact prints; prints.
   (2) Index to colour transparencies; transparency file.

E. Finds
   (1) Inventory of all finds.
   (2) The finds.

Acknowledgements.

Work was undertaken with the permission and support of Messrs. Ward, Ashcroft and Parkman (Consulting Engineers), Ribble Valley Borough Council, and the North West Water Authority. The author would like to acknowledge the generous assistance of the staff of Messrs. Kirk, the contractors, without whose help and support at all times, none of the work described here would have been possible. A particular debt of gratitude is owed to Mrs N. Dixon, then Curator of Ribchester Museum, Mr B.J.N.Edwards (Lancashire County Archaeologist) and Dr T.W.Potter (then of Lancaster University) for their constant help and support. Work was carried out by a small team assembled at extremely short notice and special thanks are due to Andy Bartlett, Kathleen Birtwistle, Carol Bownass, Peter Clegg, Stuart Eastwood, Nancy Edwards, Peg Howard, Steve Kaim-Caudle, John Lock, Helen Lockwood, Joan McDougall, Tony Pieczonka, Chris Taylor, Val Thomas, Jon Triscott, Viv Underwood, Kevin York and the members of the Ribble Archaeological Society, for their tolerance in coping with the difficult problems of emergency rescue archaeology. The finds were processed by Lindsay Robertson, and valuable assistance was also provided by Professor G.D.B.Jones (Manchester University) and Mr J.C.Scambler.

The excavation and post-excavation work was funded by a grant from the Department of the Environment and thanks are also due to the late Miss Dorothy Charlesworth for supporting the work from its inception. Facilities, services and some financial support were provided by the Department of Classics and Archaeology, Lancaster University. The coarse pottery was drawn by R.Sulima, the Samian was drawn by R.C.Turner, and the plans and sections were drawn by P.Lee. A final debt of gratitude is owed to the contributors of specialist reports.

PART A:
REPORT OF EXCAVATIONS UNDERTAKEN IN THE AREA OF MANHOLE 6.

Section 1. (Fig.9).

Section 1 was dug by machine to a depth of c.2.0 m. and yielded some quantity of samian and coarse pottery. The upper layers comprised disturbed topsoil (FN.9), and two machine disturbances resulting from the recent pipelaying work.

A pit c.1.20 m. in diameter (FN.1 layers A-E) had been cut through the redeposited natural subsoil (FN.6 + FN.12) to a depth of 80 cms. The two separate phases of silting identified within the fill (layers D-E and layers A-C) may indicate a shallow recut after the deposition of the primary fill. The entire pit was cut by a shallow parallel sided slot with a U-shaped profile, 40 cms wide and 60 cms deep (FN.3 layers A-C) which terminated in a steep butt end and with apparent wood stains along part of the south-western edge. It was only possible to excavate a short length of this feature, presumably part of a foundation trench of a timber building, although no associated floor levels were identified. The fill was

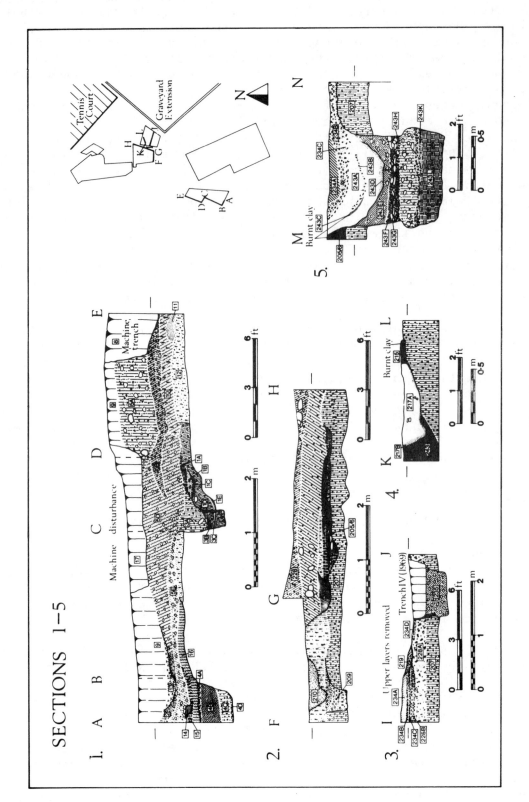

Fig.9.

fairly uniform, with a concentration of small cobbles in the upper layer (FN.3 layer A), perhaps derived from a rammed cobble floor.

To the west, a shallow deposit c. 20 cms deep (FN.15 layers A-B, and FN.16) cut the redeposited natural subsoil and immediately overlay an earlier feature (FN.4 layers A-D); both features were recorded only in section. Although not directly linked stratigraphically, FN.4 was presumably broadly contemporary with FN.1 (above), and the deposition of FN.15/16 may represent a general clearance associated with the construction of the foundation trench of a timber building (FN.3). A small feature c.20 cms wide and 15 cms deep (FN.14) cut into the surface of FN.15/16, and sealed by three flat stones may have been contemporary with those layers sealing FN.1 (FN.10 and FN.11), perhaps indicating a deliberate dumping of material in this area to level the ground surface.

These lower levels (including FN.5 layer E and FN.2) were in turn overlain by a large mixed deposit of silt, cobbles, gravel and small pebbles up to c.1.20 m thick (FN.5 layers A-D). Although separate layers within this deposit could be distinguished, it presumably represents a deliberate dump of mixed material, covering the whole area with a thick layer of gravel and cobbles. At the western end of the section a small feature containing concentrations of charcoal and burnt clay (FN.13) overlay both FN.2 and FN.5 layer D, and suggested the presence of a hearth or oven.

Section 2. (Fig.9).
Section 2 was dug by machine to a depth of c.1.0 m after the overburden of topsoil and machine disturbances had already been removed by pipelaying operations. Consequently Roman levels were encountered immediately the section was excavated. A mixed deposit of disturbed and redeposited natural subsoil c.30 cms thick included some occupation material (FN.207). A feature with a U-shaped profile (FN.209 layers A-D) cut into this layer, and may have been part of the same building or range of structures represented by FN.334 (below). A second feature also cut into FN.207 contained a high volume of burnt material (FN.205/206) and was originally thought to represent the destruction by fire of a possible timber building in the area. Limited excavation, however, demonstrated that the deposit was quite discrete, and the layers of burnt and unburnt clay and charcoal, therefore, probably indicate the presence of a small hearth or oven, associated with a stoke-hole.

A later shallow feature with a flattened U-shaped profile c.1.0 m wide and c.40 cms deep (FN.210) was cut through an intermediate deposit into the upper fill of FN.209, and may represent a small pit, part of a ditch, or part of a structure. The overlying deposit was composed of a general accumulation of mixed occupation material c.60 cms thick (FN.204 layers A-B), part of which retained a shallow ditch or pit-like profile (layer B). The entire section was sealed by a second layer of mixed occupation material which contained a fairly high proportion of small cobbles FN.228).

Section 3. (Fig.9).

It was possible to conduct some very limited excavation in the area between Section 2 and the north wall of the graveyard, in an attempt to interpret some of the features observed in that section. Unfortunately this area had already been extensively disturbed by machine activity, and the upper layers removed in order to backfill the pipe trench. Section 3 was excavated to a depth of c.0.5 m and crossed the western end of Trench IV excavated in 1969.

The disturbed and redeposited ground surface already identified in Section 2 (FN.207) was also succeeded here by a horizon of occupation material (FN.228 layer A), the surface of which was sealed by a thin deposit of mixed sand and gravel (FN.228 layer B), possibly a floor level. Part of an unexcavated pit (FN.235), cut through FN.228 into FN.207, was recorded on the floor of the 1969 trench. The surviving portion of this pit was c.1.0 m in diameter and c.45 cms deep, with a uniform fill; part of the northern edge of the pit appeared to have been deliberately lined with hard packed clay and crushed and compacted sandstone, perhaps indicating some form of industrial activity.

A second deposit of occupation material, c.10 cms thick (FN.234 layers C-D), overlay the possible floor level of FN.228, and was in turn overlain by a thin layer of crushed and compacted yellow sand and gravel (FN.234 layer B), presumably a second floor level, which was also succeeded by a further thin layer of occupation material (FN.234 layer A). A small portion of a shallow unidentifiable feature (FN.219) cut all the levels comprising FN.234, and may indicate the erosion of the later ground surface.

Section 4. (Fig.9).

Although the surface of the excavated area south of section 2 was badly disturbed by machine activity, a portion of a small hearth or oven survived, set in the surface of FN.207 and FN.243. Only a very small segment of the structure of this feature survived, composed of burnt and unburnt clay (FN.215 layers A-B). A shallow sub-rectangular pit c.60 cms long by c.30 cms wide, and c.20 cms deep (FN.217 layers A-B), was associated with this structure. The fill was a uniform silt mixed with charcoal. However, the pit was lined by a thin layer of oxidised red sand, indicating burning.

Section 5. (Fig.9).

A large pit, c.80 cms in diameter and c.1.0 m deep (FN.243 layers A-L) dug into the natural yellow clay and gravel, was excavated in the small area south of Section 2, and clearly represents several distinct phases of activity. After deposition of the lower fill (layers I-L), it probably fell out of use, whilst the occupation horizon FN.207 accumulated. A subsequent recut through FN.207 to a depth of c.60 cms occurred, and the base of the pit was deliberately lined with layers of sandstone rubble and pebbles set in clay (layers F-H). Further silting then occurred (layer E), presumably derived from the adjacent occupation horizon (FN.207). A final recut was made subsequent to the construction of a hearth or oven (FN.205/206) in the surface of FN.207 (above). This burnt clay feature was cut away by the upper portion of the pit, and material derived from it was included in the final fill of the pit (layers A-D). Part of the upper fill of the pit was overlain by a short sequence of thin occupation and possible floor levels probably belonging to the same complex described above (Section 3, FN.234).

Section 6. (Fig.10).

Section 6 was dug by machine to an average depth of c.2.0 m, and yielded large quantities of samian and coarse pottery. Much of the upper layers of the section had already been removed in order to backfill the pipe trench, although at the western end of the section the disturbed topsoil did survive.

The basal layers of the section comprised the disturbed and redeposited natural ground surface mixed with the initial accumulation of occupation material in the area (FN.307). Two simple features with pit-like profiles (FN.318 and FN.329) cut through FN.307. Although FN.318 was originally thought to represent part of the earliest phase of construction pit for the stone lined well (FN.301 layer B), its association with the well (FN.300) was doubtful, and on further examination, a small portion of a second pit (FN.341) was observed cutting through the fill of FN.318, immediately adjacent to the well. This later feature is more likely, therefore, to represent the earliest phase of well construction, post-dating the fill of FN.318, and cutting through FN.307. Unfortunately, it was not possible to excavate any of these features.

The fill of the pit FN.329 was succeeded by the apparently continuous accumulation of occupation material (FN.321 layers A-D, FN.322 layers A-D and FN.323 layers A-K), and although the material recovered from these layers is consistent in date, several distinct horizons were identified within the general deposit. FN.323 layers A-K immediately post-dated the fill of the possible pit (FN.329), and was also consistent with the fill of FN.318; the fill of the latter pit was, therefore, presumably contemporary with the deposition of FN.323. At the base of this horizon a small deposit of sand and gravel mixed with charcoal may indicate a structurally related feature. However, no further investigation was possible. Part of the surface of FN.323 was sealed by a thin layer of charcoal c.2 cms thick, prior to the construction of the early well pit.

A small flat-bottomed feature with vertical sides c.15 cms deep and c.20 cms wide, and a fill uniform with the overlying occupation material (FN.322) was cut into the surface of FN.323 and may represent a structural element. Part of the content of FN.322 had a high incidence of pebbles, suggesting the deliberate laying of a firm surface around the well. A third horizon c.60 cms thick (FN.321 layers B-D) overlay FN.322, and was sealed by a deposit of

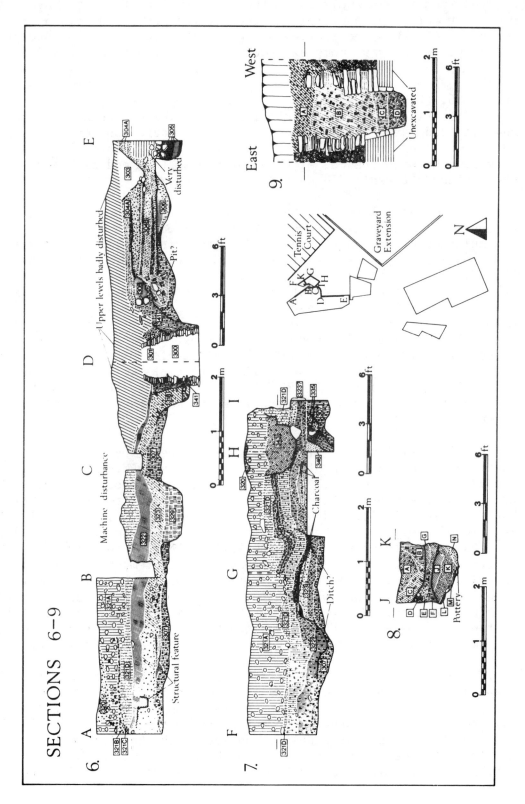

Fig.10.

large cobbles (FN.321 layer A). A shallow feature c.25 cms deep (FN.320) ran across the top of this cobble layer, and a similar feature observed in section 7 (FN.320) may have formed part of the same shallow ditch, aligned approximately north-south.

The fill of two small features cut into the surface of FN.307 (FN.305 layers A-D and FN.306 layers A-C), contained quantities of charcoal, and FN.306 also contained burnt and unburnt clay, suggesting the presence of domestic or industrial hearths or ovens in this area. Both features were sealed by alternating layers of silt and compacted small pebbles and gravel (FN.304 layer B), having the general appearance of a small road or street. A small hearth or oven (FN.308 layers A-B) was constructed in the surface of both this possible street and the fill of the earlier well construction pit (FN.301 layer B). Unfortunately the relationship between the earlier well pit, and the possible street was masked by FN.308 and a possible third pit, but suggests that the well was built after the construction of the earlier road. Additional layers of gravel and compacted pebbles (FN.304 layer A) overlay both FN.304 layer B and FN.308, and indicate a later refurbishment of the street. A feature with a V-shaped profile, presumably a ditch, (FN.303) cut through both phases of street, and must, therefore, have been dug after it fell into disuse.

A second phase of well construction pit was also identified (FN.301 layer A), cut into the earlier well pit. Unfortunately, the disturbed topsoil masked any relationship between the later well pit and any other features, and the upper layers of the section and part of the well structure itself had been badly disturbed by machine activity. The fabric of the well survived from the base of the disturbed topsoil, and it, therefore, seems likely that the upper portion would have been the latest Roman feature in the area. Certainly, the refurbished street overlay the earlier well pit and it seems likely that the second phase well pit may represent a later refurbishment of the well, which apparently remained in use throughout much of the period of Roman activity in the area.

Section 7. (Fig.10).
Section 7 was dug by machine to an average depth of c.1.6 m, after the disturbed topsoil in the area had already been removed in order to backfill the pipe trench.

A small feature, presumably a pit, (FN.347) was cut into the disturbed and redeposited natural ground surface (FN.307), and was in turn cut by a short length of possible construction trench for a wooden building (FN.335 layers A-C). A series of closely packed pebble surfaces associated with this feature possibly represent related floor levels, and large quantities of charcoal and general indications of burning in the area suggest destruction of this structure by fire. The southern edge of FN.335 was cut by a possible ditch or pit (FN.346). However, no further investigation of this feature was possible.

The later accumulation of occupation material c.30 cms thick (FN.323 layers A-I) may represent several phases of activity, including indications of pebble surfaces (layer I). The fill of two shallow possible ditches cut into the surface of FN.323 is fairly consistent with the subsequent accumulation of occupation material (FN.322 layers A-C). Alternate layers of occupation material and gravel (FN.345 layers A-D) overlay part of FN.322, and although no associated structures were identified, presumably represent floor levels. The area was then covered by a mixed layer (FN.321 layer D) into which a large pit or ditch of U-shaped profile was cut (FN.343), and then sealed by a substantial layer of silt and large cobbles (FN.321 layer A). A small shallow feature (FN.320) cut into the surface of FN.321 was probably continuous with the similar feature observed in Section 6.

Section 8. (Fig.10).
       A large pit observed in the floor of Cutting III extension (FN.319 layers A-N) was dug into the natural sand and gravel, and demonstrated several distinct phases of activity. Unfortunately this area was over-excavated by machine, and it was not possible to establish any stratigraphical relationship between the pit and any of the levels observed in Section 7. The initial gradual silting and fill (layers J-N) was followed by the apparent deliberate dumping of material onto the floor of the pit (layers D-H), followed in turn by a second gradual accumulation of material (layers A-B). It is possible that layers A and C may represent a final phase of silting after part of the upper portion of the pit was recut to a depth of c.50 cms.

SECTIONS 1-8: DISCUSSION.
       As a result of the conditions under which much of the work in this area was carried out, comparatively little of the material recovered from the site was well stratified. Large quantities of samian and coarse pottery were retrieved from the pipe trench in the area of Manhole 6 (Area C), and only a minimum of these vessels have been described or illustrated. The bulk of this unstratified pottery is dated to the first or second century A.D., although a few pieces may be later. Some of the problems of analysing a mixed collection of largely unstratified pottery have been discussed below. However, the extremely variable conditions under which this material was collected preclude any attempt to collate information here in the form of histograms.

       Unfortunately it was only possible to excavate a small number of the features revealed in Sections 1-8, and only a limited volume of datable material was recovered by this work. Consequently, detailed interpretation of these sections is difficult, and compounded by the general lack of dating evidence; nevertheless, in the area of Manhole 6, it is possible at least to identify several main phases of activity.

Phase 1.

The natural subsoil of the area is composed of mixed river gravels and sand with patches of alluvial clay. Cut into this was at least one pit (FN.243), indicating activity prior to the main phase of occupation. A general mixed basal deposit throughout the area presumably represents the disturbed and redeposited ground surface (FN.12,6,207 and 307), and broadly contemporary activity is evinced by a small hearth or oven (FN.205/206) cut in the surface of this layer.

The very small volume of material associated with these features comprises a Flavian group of samian including a stamp (no.20) together with coarse pottery (nos.217-218) including a jar (no.217) dated A.D. 80-130, all from FN.243, and scraps of Neronian or Flavian and Flavian or Trajanic samian and some late first-early second century coarse pottery (no.221). Consequently there is little direct dating evidence for Phase 1, although the samian may indicate a Flavian date, in contrast to the coarse ware which appears to be later. This primary activity probably corresponds to Phase I identified in the Playing Field (Ch.2).

Phase 2.

The earliest stage of phase 2 is represented by the cutting of several pits (FN.329,347,305,306 and 318) as well as the recut of the earlier pit (FN.243). Two short lengths of possible foundation trench (FN.209 and FN.334) may have belonged to the same building or range of structures, as may two other isolated pits (FN.319 and FN.232). In part of the area at least, this activity was followed by the accumulation of occupation material prior to the cutting of two more possible pits (FN.204 and FN.210). A second deposit of occupation material occurred in part of the area (FN.228), before the cutting of one pit (FN.235), and one possible ditch or pit (FN.346).

Virtually no datable material was recovered from most of the features described above. The construction trench and presumably contemporary pits produced some samian of Flavian and Flavian/Trajanic date, and some late first/early second century and second century coarse ware (including nos.214-215). The occupation horizon FN.228 produced Flavian or Trajanic samian, and probable pre-Hadrianic coarse pottery (nos.212-213), and the fill of the later pit FN.235 contained one piece of Antonine samian, together with assorted self coloured coarse wares of the late first/early second century (probably pre-Hadrianic), and a coin of Vespasian (no.680).

The main Roman occupation of the area began in phase 2, and consisted of a variety of features, mainly pits, together with one possible timber structure, succeeded by a general accumulation of occupation material, and the cutting of more pits. It is not possible to offer any more detailed interpretation regarding the nature and function of any of these features. The bulk of material from this phase is Flavian or Trajanic in date, and in general,

corresponds fairly closely with the early part of phase II
identified in the Playing Field (Ch.2 above).

Phase 3.

At the beginning of Phase 3, the pit FN.243 was again recut,
material was also dumped into the half silted pit FN.319, and two
new pits (FN.1 and FN.4) were apparently constructed. This activity
was followed by a general accumulation of occupation material
(FN.15/16 and FN.323). In one part of the area a street or road
(FN.304) and a well (FN343 and FN.301B) were constructed, probably
contemporary with a variety of floor levels (FN.234), and presumably
related to a timber building represented here by a short length of
construction trench (FN.3); a small hearth or oven (FN.217) may also
have been associated with this activity. A subsequent horizon of
occupation material was then deposited (FN.10/11 and FN.322),
followed by a number of possible floor levels (FN.345). A small
hearth or oven (FN.308), constructed on the surface of the street
may also belong to this later phase 3 activity, and indicates that
by this time the street had fallen into disuse.

Undoubtedly much of the material associated with this phase
was residual, derived from earlier horizons, but it also includes a
samian stamp dated c.A.D.75-90 (no.17), Hadrianic – early Antonine
and Antonine samian (no.21) together with mainly second century
coarse pottery (including nos.231-235), as well as a late first
century or early second century flagon (no.190). The levels
associated with the main phase 3 activity also produced Hadrianic or
early Antonine samian together with possible Hadrianic to Antonine
coarse pottery (nos.240-241), as well as at least one small fragment
of late second-early third century Black-burnished ware. The second,
later horizon of occupation material yielded Hadrianic and Antonine
samian (including no.30), and coarse pottery apparently belonging to
the second century. The possible floor levels overlying this horizon
contained a coin of A.D.107 (no.678).

Activity in the area during phase 3 may be sub-divided into
three stages. Initially, several pits were either dug or recut,
possibly indicating a continuation of land use from phase 2.
Following this, the area appears to have been occupied more
intensively, with the construction of at least one building and a
road; the accumulation of floor levels associated with this activity
suggests several phases of occupation, which may relate to the
slightly later construction, first of a pit, and then of the well.
The road may have fallen out of use prior to subsequent activity
represented by a second occupation horizon together with some
surviving floor levels, presumably of a second structure. Most of
the material associated with all elements of phase 3 is of Hadrianic
or early Antonine date, and corresponds broadly with the later part
of phase II identified in the Playing Field. In the area of Manhole
6, however, this phase may have continued longer into the Antonine
period than further east.

Phase 4.

At the end of phase 3 the road was apparently reconstructed on its original alignment (FN.5, layer E and FN.321,layers B-D). One pit (FN.343) cut into the road and a small occupation horizon (FN.2 and FN.321, layer C) superimposed on its surface also indicates some activity at this period. No other features associated with this phase were identified, and it is likely that most activity at this time had shifted further east.

In addition to a very small quantity of presumably residual material, the bulk of finds associated with this later road comprised early second century samian and coarse pottery (nos.236-238), including a body sherd of beaker, probably a Nene Valley product (no.239), dated to the third century A.D. The subsequent occupation horizon also contained early second century samian, including a stamp (no.24) dated c.A.D.105-125, and a decorated sherd (no.25) of Hadrianic-early Antonine date (from FN.321, layer C), as well as a largely residual group of samian (from FN.2) of which the latest material is Antonine (including no.18, dated c.A.D. 160-200). This level also contained plentiful second century coarse pottery (including nos.191-199 and 201-203) together with one sherd (no.200) which suggests that deposition did not close before the latter years of that century.

Phase 4 may be divided into two parts: the earlier deposition of the presumed new road surface, containing early second century material, and occurring soon after the latter part of phase 3 (perhaps associated with the new system of roadways described above). This road was then succeeded by faint traces of occupation, probably belonging to the second half of the second century, and although no traces of timber buildings or other more intensive activity were recorded, the general character of these deposits was fairly consistent with that of phase III identified in the Playing Field.

Phase 5.

After the slight traces of activity recorded at the close of phase 4, the entire area was sealed by a massive mixed deposit of cobbles, gravel and small pebbles, up to c.1.20 m thick (FN.5, layers A-D and FN.321, layer A); it is also possible that the well (FN.300) may have been refurbished at this time. With the exception of a small deposit of occupation material (FN.13), and two pits (FN.303 and FN.319), there was little trace of any other activity in the area, although a small feature (FN.320) cut into the surface of the cobbles may have been part of a construction trench of a later timber building.

The cobbles contained probable Antonine samian and the coarse pottery included the neck sherd of a flagon in Black-burnished ware (no.204), likely to date between the early-mid second century and the early third century, and a probable sherd of Crambeck ware (no.205) dated to c.A.D. 350-400, as well as presumably residual material redeposited with the cobbles. The well contained early Antonine samian, including one decorated piece (no.21) dated c.A.D.140-160, and coarse pottery including a beaker (no.219) dated A.D. 250-300, and a flagon in Black-burnished ware (no.220), and it, therefore, probably remained in use up to the mid third century. The coarse pottery from the pit FN.319 included a jar in Black-burnished ware (no.232) dated to the early-mid fourth century, indicating some activity at the beginning of the fourth century.

Phase 5 represents the final period of Roman activity in the area, and it is clearly related to Playing Field period IV. Although there appears to have been some slight activity at this time, no traces of furnaces were recorded and the general lack of domestic or industrial activity already noted during phase 4 appears to have continued. The well defined edge of a large deposit composed of massive cobbles was excavated close by in 1980 (Edwards and Webster 1985, p.47), and although no direct connection with FN.5 and FN.321 may be demonstrated, it is at least possible that they both form a continuation of that feature, possibly a street or road defining the southern limit of the settlement on this side of the fort.

THE PADDOCK (CUTTING IV): EXCAVATION (Fig.11).

The small area of waste land lying east of the Black Bull car park, known locally as 'The Paddock', was made available for investigation for a period of three weeks immediately prior to pipe laying operations. This plot lay in close proximity to the known location of cremation burials discovered in the 'Transport Yard' in 1967. Therefore, it was considered essential to establish whether a possible Roman cemetery might have extended north into this area. Initially, three trenches were excavated by machine along the east and west margins of the site. However, no burials were revealed although some Roman activity was demonstrated by the presence of features observed in the sections, in addition to quantities of Roman pottery recovered during this work. Topsoil was then stripped from the remainder of the available area by machine, but again, no traces of any burials were recorded, although a variety of other features were revealed. Stratigraphy in this area was relatively shallow (rarely in excess of 1.0 m deep), and the density of recorded features was also sparse; many were located in virtual stratigraphic isolation, and substantial segments of the area contained no features at all. Consequently, the detailed interpretation of Roman activity recorded here is extremely difficult, and it is only possible to make a most general assessment of the nature and chronology of the Roman occupation of this part of Ribchester.

The earliest features.

The undisturbed natural subsoil was overlain by a relatively shallow deposit representing the earliest disturbance to the natural ground surface during the Roman period (FN.600,627 and 637). At

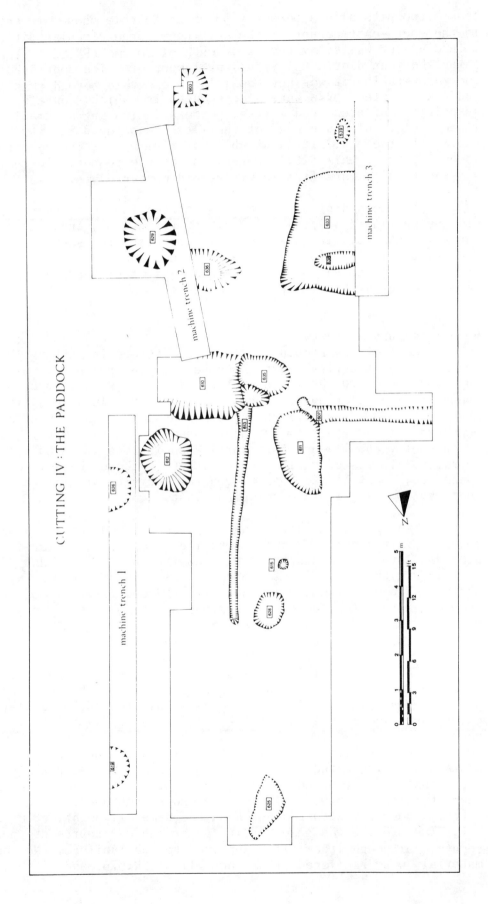

CUTTING IV: THE PADDOCK

Fig.11.

least two pits also apparently belonged to this phase of activity. In the south-east corner of the cutting a large circular pit c.1.40 m in diameter was excavated to a depth of 80 cms (FN.629). The fill comprised four distinct layers, the lowest of which continued below the water-table (it was not possible to excavate beyond this level), and was sealed by a water-logged deposit which contained large quantities of preserved wattle, perhaps indicating a small wattle lined well, although none of the wattle was found in situ at the edges of the pit. Little datable material was recovered from the lower fills of this pit. However, the coarse pottery did include a jar (no.487) of late first/early second century date.

The second pit (FN.628) was located in the northern portion of the cutting, isolated from any other features, and cut into the natural subsoil. It was roughly circular in shape, 1.0 m in diameter, with steep sides 35 cms deep, and a flat bottom. The uniform fill contained a very few scraps of pottery but no clear indication of either its purpose or date.

Second century activity.

Most of the remaining features recorded in Cutting IV may be assigned to activity during the second century A.D., with some continuation into the third century. It is, however, apparent from the chronological range of finds recovered from individual features, and from some stratigraphic relationships, that this activity occurred in at least two separate phases. Unfortunately, in the absence of virtually any horizontal associations it is not possible to relate all features with one or other of these phases. Some may, therefore, only be ascribed to general activity within the second century A.D., and will be described last.

Two fairly substantial features (FN.619 and FN.626) were observed in the eastern face of machine trench 1, associated with a general layer of disturbance c.10 cms thick (FN.617 and FN.601) similar to the initial disturbed natural ground surface described above (FN.600), although it has only produced material of general second century A.D. date. Both FN.619 and FN.626 were largely dug away by machine during excavation of the trench and consequently only the lower portion of each feature survived.

FN.619 was c.1.4 m wide and 80 cms deep, with near vertical sides and a flat bottom, and may represent either the butt end of a ditch or a pit. The lower fill was mainly formed by a layer of compressed wattle c.18 cms thick, resting directly on the natural sand, and separated from the mixed upper fill by a layer of charcoal 10 cms thick. Both the fill of FN.619 and the horizon FN.617 contained samian dated c.90-110, together with coarse pottery of the first half of the second century A.D. FN.626 was similar in character to FN.619, c.1.6 m wide and 80 cms deep, with a flat bottom, possibly either a ditch on the same alignment, or a second pit. The profile was somewhat irregular and may represent possible recuts, although the fill appeared to be uniform. No datable material was recovered from the fill of FN.626, and it is only linked to this phase of activity by its similarity to FN.619.

A shallow pit c.90 cms in diameter and 20 cms deep (FN.603) was recorded at the southern edge of the cutting, cut through FN.600 (see above) into the natural subsoil. The uniform fill contained four large stones, and may, therefore, represent the surviving portion of a large stone packed post-hole, although there were no other structural elements with which it may easily be associated. Material from the pit included samian of Hadrianic date and some coarse ware characteristic of the first half of the second century A.D.

A short length of shallow straight-sided gully 14 cms wide and 15 cms deep (FN.638) ran approximately east from the edge of machine trench 3, for a length of 1.25 m before coming to a butt end. This feature was only observed after the excavation of the later hollow, FN.633 (below), and whilst it is possible that it may have been a constituent element of that hollow, the two fills were quite distinct, presumably representing seperate activity. Material recovered from FN.638 dates from the late first to mid-second century. There are no structural elements of a building with which FN.638 may readily be related, and it could equally represent a simple drainage gully, the basal portion of an originally more substantial ditch, or a plot boundary or fence line.

The later phase of second century activity included two short lengths of straight, shallow slots with vertical sides and flat bottoms (FN.607 and FN.613). FN.607 ran approximately west-east for 3.0 m, then turned south-east before coming to an immediate butt end. Finds included two Black-burnished jars (nos.255 and 256) of late second and late third century date. The second slot (FN.613) ran approximately north-south for 6.2 m, terminating in a butt end at the north. To the south it was cut away by later activity (FN.610 and FN.635), but probably came to an end in this area. Very little material was recovered from this feature: only a single sherd of Cheshire Plain coarseware (?second century A.D.), and one piece of samian (no.30) dated c.A.D.125-150. In spite of the inconsistent dating evidence (probably the result of the small quantity of material recovered), both slots have the general appearance of foundation trenches for timber buildings, and have, therefore, been considered together because of their similar characteristics. The plan of any such structure, however, cannot be reconstructed, and the precise relationship of the two slots is difficult to ascertain, although the out-turned butt end of FN.607 may have formed an entrance. This could, however, relate to plot divisions (eg. fence lines) rather than to a building, or, indeed, the two slots may have been totally unrelated.

In the south-west corner of the cutting a large shallow rectangular pit (FN633) formed the third major feature associated with this phase. Part of this hollow was removed during the excavation of machine trench 3. However, the surviving portion was c.3.6 by 2.1 m, and 30 cms deep with a flat bottom and near vertical sides. The fill was mixed with very large quantities of charcoal and some stones, and the eastern edge was deliberately lined with large flat stone slabs. The latest samian recovered from the pit fill (no.31) may be dated c.A.D.150-170, and whilst the coarse pottery generally indicates a mid-second century deposition, it does include a sherd of probable Category 2 Black-burnished ware dated c.A.D.150-210 (no.285). In addition to the pottery, the fill also contained large quantities of iron nails, burnt material and metal working residues. This pit, therefore, probably represents some form of industrial activity or working hollow associated with a hearth or furnace (presumably destroyed by machine trench 3).

A small pit c.1.6 m in diameter and 40 cms deep (FN.612) with steep sides and a flat bottom contained a few finds of second century date including samian dated to the second half of the second century A.D., and may also be associated with this phase. The uppermost layer of the fill of the pit/well (FN.629 above) also contained material of this date, and represents some continued activity at that time.

A very small quantity of third century material was recovered from Cutting IV, and there is, therefore, some evidence for activity subsequent to the second century. However, the features described below may only be associated with a later phase on stratigraphic grounds, and consequently they may equally repres ent additional activity within the second century A.D. FN.611 formed a shallow irregular shaped pit c.2.4 by 1.3 m and 30 cms deep, with steep sides and a flat bottom, cut into the fill of FN.607. The southern end of FN.613 was obscured by a small complex of features (FN.610/635) which clearly post-dated the fill of FN.613. Unfortunately only the lower levels of both FN.610 and FN.635 survived after the area had been stripped by machine, and no detailed interpretation or description of any of these features is possible. The presence of several features in this area was only apparent after the excavation of these lowest levels. However, part of FN.610 was observed in the east face of the cutting, and at this point was at least 50 cms deep, and must, therefore, represent either a fairly substantial elongated pit, or a ditch running in an east-west direction. The original cut of this feature was fairly irregular, and FN.635 may have been an integral part of the pit or ditch (FN.610). Although the samian recovered from FN.610/635 is generally Hadrianic or early Antonine in date, the coarseware includes some piees of late second century date (nos.255 and 259), and is, therefore, consistent with the general stratigraphic position of these features.

Some features existed in almost complete stratigraphic isolation and may not readily be assigned to any phase of activity. Most of a small irregular pit or hollow (FN.636) located at the western edge of Machine trench 2 was removed during the excavation of that trench. However, the surviving portion (c.1.5 by 1.2 m and 12 cms deep) contained some burnt clay as well as a few sherds of second century pottery. Possibly the surviving portion of a small hearth, FN.636 may in fact represent no more than a silted up hollow in the Roman ground surface. At the northern end of the cutting,

FN.625 may, also represent a similar irregular hollow or shallow pit (c.1.6 m long by 80 cms wide, and c.30 cms deep). No finds were recovered from the fill of this feature at all, and it is impossible to relate it to the rest of the cutting. FN.615, a small pit c.25 cms square and 25 cms deep was similarly isolated and devoid of finds.

THE PADDOCK (CUTTING IV): DISCUSSION.

The nature of the recorded features in Cutting IV does not allow any detailed interpretation of the site. This problem is further compounded by the absence of either a horizontal or comprehensive vertical stratigraphy, resulting from the removal of the upper levels by machine in order to establish quickly the possible presence of a Roman cemetery in this area. It has, however, been demonstrated that Roman activity in this part of Ribchester may be divided into several phases of occupation.

Initial activity, represented by disturbance to the natural ground surface and the construction of two pits (one possibly a well) is dated to the late first/early second century A.D. Most features recorded, however, clearly belong to the second century, and it is possible to subdivide this occupation into an earlier and later phase. There is also some evidence for continuing use, possibly into the third century. The nature of the evidence, however, does not permit the confident subdivision into clearly defined phases, and such an attempt is only made here as a matter of descriptive convenience. The absence of recognisable buildings or clearly differentiated activities compounds these difficulties; it is likely that the area was in fairly continuous, albeit non intensive, use from the late first to the end of the second century A.D.

The interpretation of the features described also poses additional problems. The site was clearly not used for any intensive domestic occupation. Indeed, there was very little evidence for any form of domestic occupation at all. Similarly, although parts of a possible timber building may be represented by some of the features recorded, there were no indications as to the function of any such structure, and these features could just as well relate to plot or yard boundaries. The most easily interpretable feature is the rectangular pit (FN.633) which must presumably have been associated with some form of industrial activity. The presence of relatively substantial quantities of burnt clay in two of the shallow pits reinforces the possibility that this part of the civil settlement may have been devoted to such industrial activity.

The area of Cutting IV is close to the periphery of the known extent of extra-mural settlement at Ribchester, although occupation has been recorded at least 40 m further north along the line of the Roman road running north out of the village. The lack of evidence for any intensive use of the area during the Roman period is, therefore, not surprising. The area was certainly fairly open and undeveloped and at that time and may well have lain to the rear of more intensive occupation possibly represented by strip housing fronting the road. It is interesting to note that the most substantial features recorded in Cutting IV were all located along the eastern edge of the excavated area, closest to that road. In addition industrial activity would certainly have been conducted in an open area, away from more intensive domestic occupation.

PART B:
REPORT OF WATCHING BRIEF ALONG THE ROUTE OF THE PIPE TRENCH.
(Fig 8).

AREA A:MANHOLE 4(SD 6494 3483) - ANCHOR HILL(SD 6489 3495).

A permanent archaeological presence to observe the excavation of the pipe trench was only established after the trench had already been excavated and backfilled between the site of the Sewerage Works and manhole 4. No evidence of Roman activity was observed along the 100 m length of pipe trench between manhole 4 and manhole 5 (SD 6490 3492). However, between manhole 5 and Anchor Hill, there were clear indications of Roman occupation in this area. It was not possible to record in detail any of the features observed in both faces of the pipe trench, but Roman levels, including pits and fairly large deposits of occupation material, certainly existed below the topsoil, to a depth of c.1.5 m, overlying the natural subsoil. Both the samian and coarse pottery recovered from this area were first or second century A.D. in date.

It is interesting to note that although excavations on Anchor Hill in 1967 produced fourth century pottery, no material of similar date was recovered from the pipe trench in this area. The pipe trench also revealed no trace of a Roman road running from the west gate of the fort, which should have crossed it approximately at right angles.

AREA B: ANCHOR HILL - MANHOLE 5A (SD 6487 3501).

Roman levels, generally similar in character to those observed in Area A, continued along this length of pipe trench. Pottery recovered was also of first or second century date, although it included a slightly larger proportion of material dated to the latter half of the second century A.D.

AREA C: MANHOLE 5A - MANHOLE 6 (SD 6486 3506).

Area C continued to produce large quantities of Roman material. In this part of the pipe trench the opportunity arose to record features in more detail than had hitherto been possible and it is this work that is described in more detail in Part 1. Again, the unstratified pottery is all of first and second century date, with the exception of two coarse ware jars (archive) that may be later.

AREA D: MANHOLE 6 - MANHOLE 7 (SD 6484 3510).

After the work carried out in Area C, no further opportunities arose to conduct detailed recording along the pipe trench in this area of Ribchester, and the available resources were concentrated on the excavation of the Paddock. One complex of features (FN.315 and FN.317) located at the southern end of this length of pipe trench was, however, recorded in a little more detail as part of the general work on Area C. The finds from these features have been described within the relevant specialist reports under the heading of Cutting III. A large pit (FN.315) was observed in the northern face of manhole pit 6, at least 1.0 m in diameter and 1.5 m deep, with a fill of dark, very organic silt. It was not possible to record or excavate this feature adequately, and pottery was only recovered from the fill during excavation of the pipe trench by machine. The material recovered did, however, include large quantities of Dressel 20 amphorae and indeed, the pit appeared to have been deliberately lined with large slabs of previously broken amphorae. A stamped amphora handle from the pit (no.223) may be dated to the second half of the first century A.D., although other material from the same context (including samian) is characteristic of the Antonine period.

A group of small pits and horizontal layers (collectively described as FN.317) was seen in the west face of this section of pipe trench, apparently overlying and cut into the surface of the pit described above. No detailed work on these features was possible, and the finds described as belonging to the FN.317 complex should generally be regarded as unstratified. The coarse ware in particular forms a mixed group of second - fourth century date. This does, however, reinforce the impression that these features are later than the pit (FN.315), and the presence of third and fourth century material may indicate the presence of later activity in this part of Ribchester.

Several more large pits, similar to FN.315, were observed along the line of the pipe trench in Area D, c.3.0-4.0 m apart. Unfortunately, it did not prove possible to record these features in any detail, however, large quantities of pottery including Dressel 20 amphorae, were recovered from this area. This material was generally of first and second century date with a few later exceptions (see archive). These features were almost undoubtedly large refuse pits containing material presumably derived from a nearby area of fairly intensive domestic occupation in use during the second century A.D.

AREA E: MANHOLE 7 - MANHOLE 10 (SD 6500 3525).

Only intermittent traces of Roman activity were observed along this 230 m length of pipe trench, interspersed with areas containing no evidence for Roman occupation at all. The main feature observed was a second stone built well (FN.700) at SD 6491 3516, cut c.2.0 m deep into the natural yellow sand and gravel. Conditions were such that no recognisable construction pit for this well was identified, and it was only possible to draw the section across the well itself (Section 9, Fig.10).

The lowest fill of the well (layer D) was c.40 cms thick, with a high organic content, presumably representing silting and disturbance at the base of the well shaft, and contained very few finds, although it did include one sherd of Black-burnished ware. Overlying this basal fill was a second layer c.25 cms thick (layer C) also mixed with organic material, which contained large quantities of finds, including pottery, and at least two thirds of a wooden barrel and several leather sandals. When first uncovered, the barrel comprised two semi-circular pieces of wood pegged together with at least one wooden pin. Four staves of the barrel survived in an upright position and were attached to, and kept in place by an almost complete iron hoop. The remaining pieces of the barrel were scattered immediately around their original position and had presumably been broken away by the machine excavating the pipe trench. Most of the leather was found inside the barrel and faint traces of cord were also observed (unfortunately it was not possible to recover the cord). The wood and leather were in an excellent state of preservation as a result of the waterlogged conditions. Both the samian and coarse pottery from this layer indicate a second century date. Wood and leather objects will form the subject of a report in Part 4 of this series.

Most of the upper portion of the well fill consisted of a single layer c.1.3 m thick (layer C), containing very little material and probably representing a long period of natural silting after the well had fallen out of use. A layer of disturbed plough soil sealed the top of the well, and lay immediately below the topsoil (layer A).

Although no other specific features were recorded in detail in area E, it is interesting to note that Roman activity appeared to occur within fairly well defined bands along this length of the pipe trench (including an extensive organic deposit composed mainly of straw, in the area of SD 6498 3522). This is entirely consistent with the probable ribbon development of the outlying parts of the civil settlement, along roads or streets running north from the fort, and described elsewhere in this volume. It should be noted, however, that it was not possible to identify the roadway excavated in the Playing Field car park in 1973. Material recovered from Area E is of late first and second century date, and this is also consistent with the general dating of other parts of the settlement excavated in this area.

RIBCHESTER VILLAGE STREETS.
In addition to the work described above, observation continued during pipe-laying operations along the village streets. Although it was not possible to undertake any detailed recording, Roman material was recovered from most parts of the pipe trench in the village. It was usually impossible even to gain an impression of the original context of this material. In many cases, the pipe trench clearly ran along the line of earlier mains service trenches,

the material recovered may, therefore, have been redeposited.
of this material (deposited in Ribchester Museum) has been
nented on.

During 1978, the final stretch of pipe trench was excavated
ween Anchor Holme (SD 6503 3494) and the Rectory gates (SD 6506
4). This area lies inside the fort, close to the known location
both the **principia** and the **praetorium**. Observation of this work
also extremely difficult. However, it was possible to record the
sence of dressed masonry, and at least one hearth-like stucture.
erial recovered during this observation included quantities of
fing tile, and a small mixed group of samian and coarse wares
ing from the late first to the late second century A.D.

LD NUMBER CATALOGUE

	Category	Cutting/Area	Date/Phase
1	Pit: layers A-E.	I	3
2	Horizon: ?same as FN.13.	I	4
3	Foundation trench?: layers A-C.	I	3
4	?Pit: layers A-D.	I	3
5	Mixed cobble horizon: layers A-E.	I	4-5
6	Redeposited natural subsoil.	I	1
7	Unstratified	I	
8	Machine intrusion.	I	
9	Disturbed topsoil.	I	
10	Horizon.	I	3
11	Horizon.	I	3
12	Redeposited natural subsoil.	I	1
13	Horizon including hearth or oven?	I	5
14	Small pit?	I	
15	Horizon: layers A-B.	I	3
16	?Same as FN.15 (horizon).	I	3
17	Recent disturbance.	I	
18	Possible small hearth.	I	
19	?Part of hearth (FN.18).	I	
20	Part of ? pit (FN.4).	I	
21	Same as FN.20 layer A.	I	
22	Natural subsoil.	I	
23	Part of foundation trench (FN.4)	I	
24	Same as FN.20 layer B.	I	
25	Natural subsoil.	I	
26	Same as FN.20 layer C.	I	
.500– .525	Field numbers assigned during the excavation of Cutting I extension	unstratified	
.200	Part of road (FN.304).	II	
.201	Part of horizon (FN.228).	II	
.202	Same as FN.204, layer A (horizon).	II	
.203	Part of horizon (FN.228).	II	
.204	Horizon: layers A-B, includes pit/ditch	II	2

	Category	Cutting/Area	Date/Phase
FN.205	?Stoke-hole of hearth/oven(FN.206).	II	1
FN.206	?Hearth/oven.	II	1
FN.207	Horizon.	II	1
FN.208	Same as FN.209 layer D	II	
FN.209	?Foundation trench: layers A-D	II	2
FN.210	?Pit/ditch/foundation trench.	II	2
FN.211-3	Part of backfill (FN.233).	II	
FN.214	Part of horizon (FN.228).	II	
FN.215	?Hearth or oven: layers A-B.	II	3?
FN.216	Same as FN.217	II	
FN.217	?stoke-hole of FN.215: layers A-B.	II	3?
FN.218	Part of horizon (FN.228).	II	
FN.219	?Erosion feature.	II	
FN.220	Surface/horizon.	II	
FN.221	?Part of horizon (FN.228).	II	
FN.222	Insubstantial surface.	II	
FN.223	Part of backfill (FN.233).	II	
FN.224	?Part of road (FN.304).	II	
FN.225	Same as FN.214 (horizon).	II	
FN.226	Topsoil.	II	
FN.227	Part of backfill (FN.233).	II	
FN.228	Horizon: layers A-B.	II	2
FN.229	Part of horizon (FN.228).	II	
FN.230	Part of backfill (FN.233).	II	
FN.231	?Part of pit (FN.232).	II	
FN.232	Pit.	II	2
FN.233	Backfill of 1969 excavation.	II	
FN.234	Horizon: layers A-D.	II	3
FN.235	Large pit.	II	2
FN.236	Part of horizon (FN.228).	II	
FN.237	Part of horizon (FN.228).	II	
FN.238	Same as FN.243,layer A.	II	
FN.239	Same as FN.243,layer B.	II	
FN.240	Same as FN.243,layer C.	II	
FN.241	Same as FN.243,layer D.	II	
FN.242	Same as FN.243,layers E-G.	II	
FN.243	Large pit: layers A-I.	II	1-3
FN.244	Same as FN.243,layers H-I.	II	
FN.300	Well.	III	3-5
FN.301	Construction pit of well (FN.300).	III	3
FN.302	Unassigned.		
FN.303	?Ditch.	III	5
FN.304	Road/street.	III	3
FN.305	?Hearth/oven: layers A-D.	III	2
FN.306	?Hearth/oven: layers A-C.	III	2
FN.307	Redeposited natural subsoil.	III	1
FN.308	Hearth/oven: layers A-B.	III	3
FN.309	Same as horizon FN.321, layers A-B.	III	
FN.310	Same as horizon FN.321, layer D.	III	
FN.311	Unassigned.		
FN.312	Part of horizon (FN.322).	III	

Category	Cutting/Area	Date/Phase
FN.313	Part of horizon (FN.345).	III	
FN.314	Unassigned.		
FN.315	Pit.	III	2'nd C
FN.316	Unassigned.		
FN.317	Mixed horizons.	III	2-4 C
FN.318	Pit: layers A-C.	III	2
FN.319	Large pit: layers A-N.	III	2-5
FN.320	?Ditch.	III	5
FN.321	Mixed horizon: layers A-D.	III	4-5
FN.322	Horizon: layers A-D.	III	3
FN.323	Horizon: layers A-K.	III	3
FN.324-5	Redeposited natural.	III	
FN.326	Part of horizon (FN.321).	III	
FN.327	Cancelled.		
FN.328	Same as horizon FN.322,layer A.	III	
FN.329	?Pit: layers A-B.	III	2
FN.330-3	Redeposited natural.	III	
FN.334	?Destruction horizon.	III	2
FN.335	?Foundation trench: layers A-C.	III	
FN.336	Same as FN.334.	III	
FN.337	?Construction slot.	III	
FN.338	Post-hole.	III	
FN.339	Redeposited natural.	III	
FN.340	Same as FN.322,layer A (horizon).	III	
FN.341	Early well pit (for FN.300).	III	3
FN.342	?Same as FN.323 (horizon).	III	
FN.343	?Foundation trench.	III	3
FN.342	Same as FN.342 (horizon).	III	
FN.345	?Floor levels: layers A-D.	III	3
FN.346	Pit or ditch: layers A-B.	III	2
FN.347	Pit ?part of FN.346 (pit or ditch).	III	2
FN.348-354	Complex of closely packed stone/ pebble surfaces (?floor levels).	III	
FN.600	Disturbed natural subsoil.	IV	L1/E2 C
FN.601	?Redeposited natural subsoil.	IV	2'nd C
FN.602	Same as FN.602 (pit)	IV	
FN.603	?Post-hole.	IV	2'nd C
FN.604	Modern disturbance.	IV	
FN.605	Modern disturbance.	IV	
FN.606	Unassigned.	IV	
FN.607	?Foundation trench/slot.	IV	2'nd C
FN.608	Part of FN.601 (horizon).	IV	
FN.609	Modern disturbance.	IV	
FN.610	Pit or ditch.	IV	3'rd C?
FN.611	Irregular pit: layers A-B.	IV	3'rd C?
FN.612	Pit: layers A-B.	IV	2'nd C
FN.613	?Foundation trench/slot.	IV	2'nd C
FN.614	Modern disturbance.	IV	
FN.615	Small pit.	IV	
FN.616	Cancelled.		
FN.617	?Redeposited natural subsoil.	IV	2'nd C

	Category	Cutting/Area	Date/Phase
FN.618	Natural subsoil.	IV	
FN.619	Pit or ditch: layers A-B.	IV	2'nd C
FN.620	Natural subsoil.	IV	
FN.621	Disturbed topsoil.	IV	
FN.622	Disturbed topsoil.	IV	
FN.623	Same as FN.629,layer A (pit)	IV	
FN.624	Same as FN.629,layer A (pit)	IV	
FN.625	Irregular hollow/pit.	IV	
FN.626	Pit or ditch.	IV	2'nd C
FN.627	Disturbed natural subsoil.	IV	L1/E2 C
FN.628	Pit.	IV	L1/E2 C
FN.629	Pit/?well: layers A-D.	IV	L1/2 C
FN.630	Disturbed natural.	IV	
FN.631	Same as FN.610,layer A (pit/ditch).	IV	
FN.632	Same as FN.610,layer B (pit/ditch).	IV	
FN.633	Work area.	IV	2'nd C
FN.634	?Part of FN.612 (pit).	IV	
FN.635	?Same as FN.610 (pit/ditch).	IV	3'rd C?
FN.636	Irregular pit/hollow: ?hearth	IV	
FN.637	Disturbed natural subsoil.	IV	L1/E2 C
FN.638	Gully.	IV	2'nd C
FN.639	?Pit.	IV	
FN.700	Stone built well: layers A-F.	E	2'nd C

Chapter 4
EXCAVATIONS IN ADVANCE OF SHELTERED HOUSING ACCOMMODATION, PARSONAGE AVENUE, RIBCHESTER, 1980.
by A.C.H.Olivier & R.C.Turner.

Introduction.

In 1979, planning approval was granted for the construction of a Sheltered Housing Scheme at the western end of Parsonage Avenue, Ribchester. The area scheduled for development was a rectangular plot of land (c.40 x 50 m) forming the north-east corner of the field centred at SD 6481 515. Excavation in advance of construction was undertaken by the Cumbria and Lancashire Archaeology Unit, on behalf of the Department of the Environment, in February and March 1980.

The site lies c.200 m north-west of the Roman fort, to the West of the road running north from the **porta principalis sinistra** (fig.12). Trial trenching in 1973, in advance of construction of the Playing Field car park (area centred SD 6489 3518 see Chapter 5) proved the line of this road, as well as demonstrating slight indications of buildings, presumably representing ribbon development north of the fort, during the first and second centuries A.D. Trial excavations in the Playing Field in 1969, north of the graveyard wall (area centred SD 6489 3511 see Chapter 2 above) also established the presence of part of the extra-mural settlement in this area between the early/mid Flavian and the later Antonine periods (See Chapter 2). This extensive settlement is, therefore, generally dated to the first and second centuries A.D., although the fort itself was continuously occupied to the late third or fourth century, and indications of any substantial post-second century activity outside the fort remained slight. The site of the sheltered housing scheme lay at the very edge of the known settlement and it was considered important to establish whether any later activity may have been located in this area.

The area scheduled for development was devoted to permanent pasture and contained no visible evidence of previous activity other than post-medieval straight ridge and furrow, which must have levelled any earlier upstanding features. In August 1978, resistivity and magnetometer survey was undertaken, and the results of both methods showed anomalies within the area to be investigated. No clearly defined features were apparent, however, and the results from the two methods were mutually exclusive. These anomalies may therefore have been either artifacts of the display, or the result of non-archaeological variations during the survey. The geophysical survey was conducted by the authors with the assistance of Dr B.K.Robinson (Department of Environmental Sciences, Lancaster University) and Mr P.Gibbons. Survey data was processed by the Ancient Monuments Laboratory (Fortress House, 23 Savile Row, London), and all data and results have been deposited in the site archive.

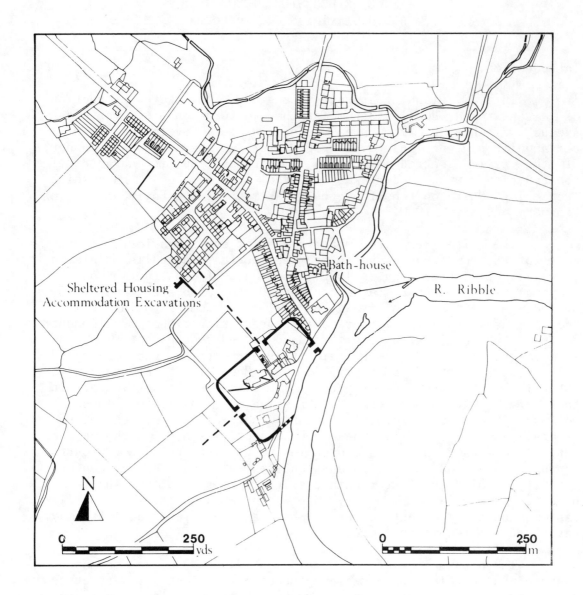

Fig.12.

In September 1979, trial trenching by machine was undertaken in order that the Unit, in conjunction with the architects and site engineers, could investigate the general archaeological potential of the site and the geophysical anomalies described above. The results of this work demonstrated that the greater part of the area to be developed included no observable archaeological features, and that the disturbed subsoil lay directly over natural riverine sands, gravels and clays. Similarly, all the geophysical anomalies explored proved to be non-archaeological in nature. However, two trenches excavated by machine across the projected line of easement for mains services (running south-east from the site along the edge of the field), did disclose fairly substantial Roman deposits to a depth, in places, of c.2 m.

Subsequent to the trial trenching, an auger survey was undertaken, in order to establish the limits of these deposits. This work demonstrated that whilst apparently Roman levels were fairly continuous along the line of easement, they only extended into the southern fringe of the main area to be developed, and soon gave way to the natural subsoil noted during trial trenching. The site of the sheltered housing accommodation, therefore, lay on the very edge of presumed settlement in this part of Ribchester. Consequently it was decided that an area comprising the southern edge of the projected development together with the line of easement (leading south towards the area of intensive occupation examined in 1969 and 1976) should be fully excavated in order to characterise the nature of Roman activity here, as well as examine the physical limits of the known settlement.

An area of 230 square metres was excavated to an average depth of c.2 m by a team of six volunteers for six weeks in February and March 1980 (fig.13). All finds from the excavation are to be deposited with the Lancashire County Museum Service. The original site archive will be deposited at the Lancashire Record Office; a copy of the full archive is retained at the Cumbria and Lancashire Archaeology Unit, University of Lancaster, and microfiche copies of the archive will be deposited at the National Monuments Record and the Lancashire County Museums Service.

Summary of Archive Contents

A. (1) Published Report.
   (2) Full report from which the published report has been abstracted. It includes the description of all excavated features together with the analysis and listing of all selected and bulk finds.

B. Site Records
   (1) Context records containing the description of all features.
   (2) Selected Finds records.
   (3) Bulk Finds records.
   (4) Site indices: Sections, Photographs.

      (5)   Surveying notes.
      (6)   Trial trench results.

C. Drawings and sections
      (1)   Original plan drawings.
      (2)   Original section drawings.

D. Photographs
      (1)   Monochrome photographs: negatives and contact prints.
      (2)   Colour transparencies.

E. Finds
      (1)   Inventory of all finds.
      (2)   The finds.

F. Radiocarbon Dating results

G. Geophysical and Auger Survey
      (1)   Magnetometer and Resistivity survey data.
      (2)   Processed data.
      (3)   Plan and results of auger survey.

ACKNOWLEDGEMENTS.

Work was undertaken with the permission of the Eaves Brook Housing Association, Cassidy and Ashton Partnership (architects), Ribble Valley Borough Council, and Mr Bolton of Hareden Hall farm. The authors would like to acknowledge in particular Mr R.G.Sutcliffe (Eaves Brook Housing Association Ltd) and Mr D.H.Bennet (Cassidy and Ashton Partnership) for their generous assistance and enthusiastic support of the project. Special thanks are also due to all the volunteers who participated in the work, and to the residents of Parsonage Avenue, Ribchester for their toleration and help during the excavations.

The excavation and post-excavation work was funded by a grant from the Department of the Environment, and thanks are also due to the late Miss Dorothy Charlesworth (Inspector of Ancient Monuments), who supported the work from its inception. A particular debt of gratitude is owed to the contributors of specialist reports. In addition we would like to thank David Breeze, Ben Edwards, Peter Webster and John Williams for their advice, comments and assistance in various matters. The plans and sections were drawn by R.C.Turner and P.Lee. Finally we would like to thank Mrs Kay Whitehead who typed the report, and whose untiring administrative support contributed to the smooth and efficient running of the project.

THE EXCAVATION (FIGS 13-18).

Period 1. Pre-Roman Activity (Fig.13).
The earliest features recorded were a series of five Bronze

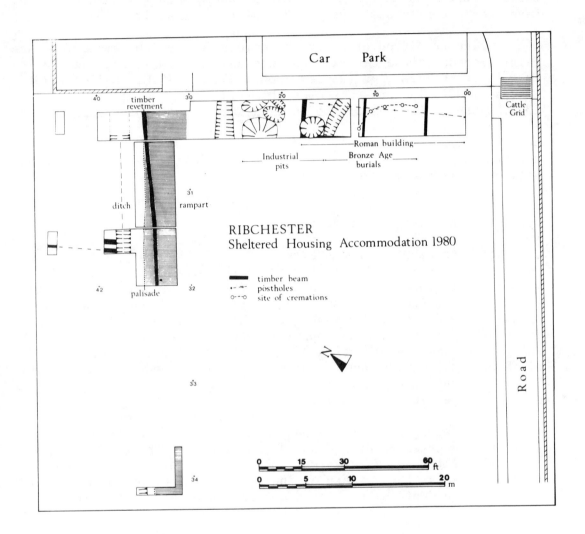

Fig.13. General Plan.

Age cremation burials (contained within collared urns), lying in an arc concentric to, and enclosed by, a presumably contemporary circular ditch, located within the southern portion of the easement trench. These burials were first observed during the removal of the floor level associated with the timber building described below and it is likely that they were not only disturbed during the Roman period, but also that some additional burials on the same arc may have been entirely destroyed by Roman or later activity.

The tradition of circular enclosed cremation cemeteries was fairly common in the central Pennines and North-west England during the later Bronze Age (Radley 1966, Hallam 1970, Bu'lock 1961, Burgess 1980). The presence of such a ring-work radiocarbon dated to 1300 BC uncal. (HAR 4443: RB80 67) in the lowlands of the region at Ribchester is obviously of considerable interest. However, this is not the appropriate place to describe or discuss these features in detail, and the full excavation report relating to these burials will be published elsewhere.

Period 2. The Earliest Roman Features.

a) Miscellaneous Ditches and Pits

The earliest Roman activity on the site was represented by a number of features located in the northern portion of the easement trench, which included a small group of pits and two short lengths of separate ditches. The most substantial of these features was a ditch (96), running in an approximately east-west direction across the trench, immediately north of the industrial pits (fig.13). This ditch was c.1 m wide and 50 cms deep, with a U-shaped profile cut into the natural subsoil, filled by a fairly uniform grey sandy clay mixed with pebbles (145. fig.16,A-B).

A second ditch (134) presumably belonging to this phase of activity was observed at the northernmost end of the easement trench (fig.17). Although it was not possible to excavate a complete section across this feature, the ditch was c.90 cms wide, and survived to a depth of c.20 cms, cut into the natural subsoil, with a flat bottom and gently shelving sides, and a uniform grey clayey silt fill mixed with pebbles (134/158 fig.18,F-G).

The largest of the early pits (160) underlay the rampart in the northern part of the easement trench just to the north of the ditch described above (96). The surviving portion of this pit was c.2.40 m in diameter, and 50 cms deep, with a flattened bottom and gently sloping sides, dug into the natural subsoil. The fill (159) was a uniform soft grey clayey silt mixed with sand and small pebbles (fig.18,F-G).

At least four other pits underlying later features also probably belonged to this stratigraphically early phase of Roman activity. A small oval pit (95. fig.15) 2.40 m long and 1.00 m wide, and surviving to a depth of 30 cms, immediately underlay a later, possibly industrial pit (21). The early pit had gently shelving sides, and the fill (94) was composed of wet grey clayey silt mixed with small stones and some charcoal. Contexts 141 and 97 may represent a similar early pit 3.00 m long by 1.60 m wide, dug into the natural gravel to a depth of 50 cms, and also immediately underlying a later pit (63). This was not, however, apparent during excavation as a result of the mixed nature of the fills of these features, and although such a distinction is suggested by the pottery, the exact relationship between these contexts was difficult to define. It is possible that pits 95 and 161 may both be integral components of the later pits 21 and 63 respectively.

Two other small pits in this area were entirely devoid of finds, but may be assigned to this phase on stratigraphic grounds (136 and 99). Pit 136 was circular, c.90 cms in diameter and 40 cms deep, cut into the natural gravel, with a uniform fill of grey clayey silt mixed with small pebbles (fig.15). Pit 99 was subrectangular in plan, c.80 cms long by 60 cms wide, also cut into the natural gravel, but only 20 cms deep, with fairly steep sides. Although much of its fill comprised a coarse grey clayey silt mixed with small pebbles, the base was lined by a thin layer of black silt mixed with pebbles and containing quantities of charcoal. There were no structural features of any form associated with the pit, but the presence of this burnt material possibly indicates use as a simple hearth. A number of other small pits and depressions in the natural gravel were also excavated in this general area; none, however, contained any finds, and all were stratigrahically isolated, and it is equally likely that they could belong to this or subsequent phases of activity.

With the exception of the possible hearth (99) there was no evidence regarding the function of any of the pits that belonged to this phase. In the absence of any appreciable quantity of material from any of these features, it is certain that they were not domestic refuse pits; their true purpose, however, remains elusive. The very limited area available for excavation also hindered any interpretation of the two small ditches associated with this early phase. However, it is interesting to note that both ditches ran on approximately the same alignment as the later defences and may, therefore, possibly represent earlier boundaries.

The small volume of material recovered from these early Roman features included coarse ware dated A.D.80-120/130 (nos.301-302) from the pit 161/97. The horizons associated with the use of the early pits (66 and possibly also 50 & 62) produced a flagon (no.300) dated A.D.70-110 and rusticated beaker (no.303) dated A.D.80-130 together with South Gaulish samian of Flavian date (no.51), as well as pre-Antonine samian (no.52), but including at least one Antonine piece (no.53). This activity is, therefore, generally pre-Hadrianic in date, spanning the years c.A.D.70/80 - c.A.D.120.

b) The Roman Timber Building (Fig.14).
A large portion of the ground plan of a presumably fairly substantial Roman timber building was recorded in the southern part

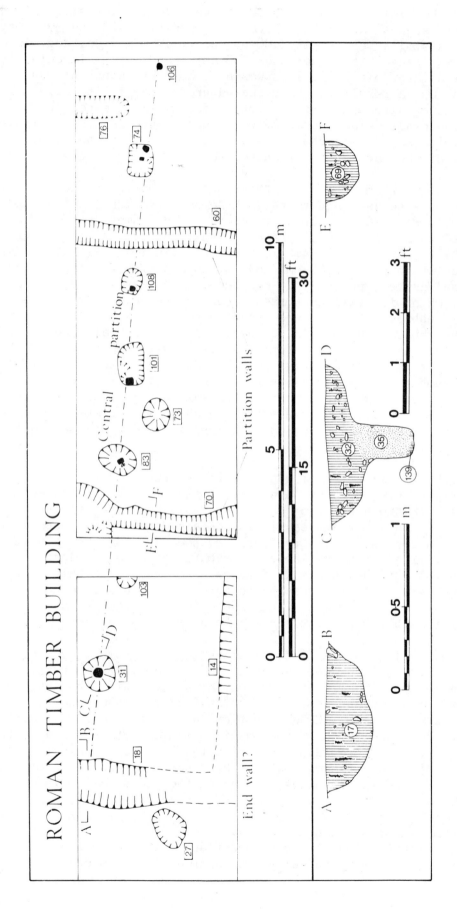

Fig.14.

of the easement trench, overlying the Bronze Age burials. Although it was not possible to recover the complete ground plan of this building, lengths of one end and one side wall were excavated, as well as internal partition walls, a row of post-holes, and various ancillary features. It is not possible to estimate the length of the building as the southern end wall must have lain outside the excavated area. However, if the line of post-holes discussed below represents a central partition, then the structure was at least c.8.00 m wide.

The northern end wall of the building was composed of a short length of construction trench c.2.50 m long, c.85 cms wide, and 35 cms deep, with fairly steep sides and a slightly flattened bottom (18). A slight shelf running along the foot of the southern edge of the trench may indicate the original position of a timber sill beam. No other trace of such timbers survived, and the fill (17) was a uniform coarse grey brown silt with iron staining (fig.16,A-B). Part of the western side wall (14) was also identified running approximately north-south along the western edge of the excavated area. It was not possible to excavate a full section across this feature. However, its dimensions appeared fairly consistent with those of the end wall described above (18). The construction trench was c.25 cms deep, with a flat bottom and steep sides. The fill (13) was a uniform coarse grey brown silt with iron staining identical to 17 (above). The junction between the side and end walls was entirely destroyed by a later intrusive pit. The similarity between both trenches, and their relationship with the other component parts of the structure leave little room for doubt that they formed part of the same substantial timber building.

Two small trenches inside the presumed structure running east-west and parallel to the end wall were presumably foundations for internal partitions. The northern partition trench was 40 cms wide and 20 cms deep, with a U-shaped profile (69/70. fig.14,E-F). The fill (69) was a uniform brown sandy silt mixed with pebbles and some iron staining. The general character of the second partition trench (60) was similar, c.45 cms wide and 25 cms deep, although the fill (61) included pieces of roofing slate.

A line of five fairly substantial post construction pits ran down the length of the structure from the northern end wall to the edge of the excavated area. Two of these (31 and 101) contained settings for large, presumably squared timbers, c. 28 x 24 cms and 16 x 20 cms respectively, whilst the remainder (83,108, and 74) contained settings for slightly smaller posts, also presumably squared, but c.12 x 16 cms. No trace of timbers survived, and the fill of all the post-pipes was a uniform orange brown silt, which underlay the upper fill of the post-pits: a grey sandy silt mixed with small pebbles and iron pan. The physical conformation of the post construction pits was varied; 31 consisted of a large subrectangular post-setting c.54 cms deep, set in a shallow circular pit c.85 cms in diameter and only 20 cms deep, whilst 101 was c.51 cms deep, in a shallow rectangular pit c.1.00 m long by 62 cms wide and 16 cms deep. Of the post-pits containing smaller post-settings, 83 was a shallow oval pit c.96 by 68 cms and 14 cms deep with a post-setting c. 59 cms deep; 108 included a post-setting 55 cms deep in a small oval pit c.60 cms long by 48 cms wide and 14 cms deep, and 74 contained two separate post-settings, 33 and 63 cms deep respectively, indicating the replacement of this particular timber upright during the life of the building. The southernmost post-setting in this line (106) was 42 cms deep, but was not associated with any surviving trace of a surrounding pit. The absence of a visible post-pipe in the upper fill of the pits could suggest that the timber posts were deliberately slighted in situ, and the resulting surface depressions or small pits filled and levelled preparatory to the next phase of activity, although this need not necessarily have been the case (Reynolds & Barber, 1984, p.99). It is also possible that, as in the case of 106 (and some examples on the Playing Field), all the posts may have been driven directly into the ground without the aid of construction pits (Manning 1981, 168-169ff.). The lack of any substantial packing around the posts could indicate that the pits resulted from the removal or slighting of the uprights rather than from their construction, although in this instance, the pits (Reynolds & Barber 1984, p.99) would probably be more irregular than those recorded here.

It should also be noted that the alignment of the row of posts converged slightly with that of the side wall and consequently they may represent an element of an entirely separate structure. Unfortunately the horizontal stratigraphy in this part of the site was insubstantial and it was not possible to demonstrate satisfactorily any such chronological distinction. The posts may, therefore, relate either to an earlier or later phase of activity. However, their general spatial relationship with the construction trenches suggests that, in spite of the use of individual posts here rather than the construction trenches favoured elsewhere in the building, they formed a central (and structural) partition to that building, and have been considered as such.

The line of posts and the two internal partitions divided the floor plan of this proposed structure into at least six regular and presumably equal-sized rooms, with internal measurements of c.6.00 by 3.00 m. In addition to the elements described above, there were also several ancillary features. A short length of a presumed foundation trench (76) ran parallel to the partition walls, from the eastern end of the excavated area for 1.50 m before termination. This trench was c.32 cms wide and 24 cms deep with a fill of grey sandy silt (77), and possibly represents an additional internal wall or partition. There were also two shallow circular pits inside the structure; the first (103) was c.49 cms in diameter, with a fill of grey sandy silt mixed with pebbles and may possibly have been another post pit, slightly offset from those described above. However, part of this pit lay underneath the baulk, and no post-pipe was recorded. The second pit (73) was 80 cms in diameter, and only 7 cms deep, and also contained a grey sandy silt (71). The only identifiable surviving floor level associated with this structure lay in the western half of the building and comprised a soft grey clayey silt. The level of the old ground surface must have been higher in the eastern half of the excavated area, and this has resulted in the removal by post-Roman activity of the upper levels of all the features associated with the building (including most of the floor level).

The absence of a complete ground plan of this structure limits any interpretation of its function. No hearth, distinctive floor levels, or appreciable quantities of domestic debris were recorded, and, although the absence of such data may be the result of post-Roman erosion, there is consequently little or no evidence that the building served a domestic function. Similarly, the lack of specialised features (kilns, hearths, etc.) and industrial waste suggests that the building was not industrial in nature. Neither do the structural elements recorded conform closely to the requirements of other specialised activities (eg.stable or grain store), although general and non-specific storage should not be ruled out as a likely or possible function.

No general occupation material or building debris was found, with the exception of the tile packing the internal partition (60), and the structure may have been deliberately demolished. Very little datable material was recovered from any of the features associated with the building although the presence of one sherd of black burnished ware may suggest a post-Hadrianic date.

Period 3. The Industrial Pits and Gullies. (Fig.15).

To the north of the timber building, a group of large pits and two gullies was recorded overlying the early pits described above, and were separated from them by at least two fairly substantial horizons (66 and 143: fig.16,A-B) which must have accumulated after the silting of the early ditch (96/145), but prior to the excavation of the later pits. Two additional horizons associated with these layers probably represent disturbed ground surfaces (50 and 142: fig.16, A-B), and indicate at least two intermediate phases of activity. Unfortunately these only survived in a limited area, and could not be directly related to either the earlier pits or the timber building described above. The presence of these horizons suggests that whilst the earlier activity may have been broadly contemporary, it is certainly most unlikely that all the features described above were in use at the same time.

It has already been seen that in two instances, a later pit immediately overlay an earlier pit of similar dimensions, and that these may all have belonged to the same general phase of activity. The ceramic evidence does, however, indicate two distinct chronological phases, also suggested by the accumulation of horizontal deposits in this area, overlying the early ditch (96/145). It is through these layers (50,62,66,142 and 143: fig.16,A-B), perhaps contemporary with the earlier pits and the building, that the later pits and gullies described here were probably cut.

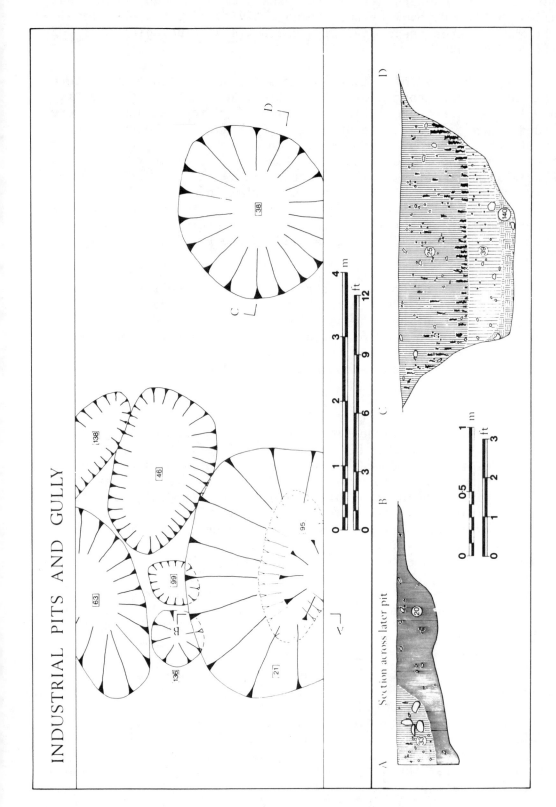

INDUSTRIAL PITS AND GULLY

Fig.15.

The southernmost pit of the group (38) was cut through the corner of the structure described above, into the natural gravel subsoil, and could, therefore, only have been dug after the building was no longer standing. This pit was roughly circular in shape with a diameter of c.2.70 m, having fairly steep sides, c.95 cms deep, and a flat bottom c.50 cms in diameter; the fill was composed of three distinct layers (25,39 and 140: fig.5,C-D). The base of the pit appeared slightly undercut, and was deliberately lined by a layer of soft grey clay (140) c.10 cms thick. The lower layer of fill proper (39) was 30 cms thick and composed of a uniform coarse grey clayey silt mixed with small pebbles. The upper fill (25) of coarse grey sandy silt mixed with small pebbles was c.55 cms thick. A concentration of iron pan was apparent at the base of this layer, and this may indicate that after the initial silting (39), the pit remained open, or in use, for some time prior to the final silting represented by context 25.

A similar sequence was observed in the large oval pit (46), lying a few metres to the north. This pit measured c.2.50 by 1.69 m, with gently shelving sides and a flat bottom c.1.00 m deep. The basal layer (45) was composed of very mixed, multi-coloured, puddled clays c.15 cms thick, and mixed with small pebbles and charcoal (44), similar to the basal layer of pit context 38. The upper fill was divided into a layer of coarse brown sandy silt mixed with small pebbles (41) 15 cms thick, underlying the main fill of coarse grey sandy silt mixed with pebbles, c.55 cms thick, which also contained a layer of iron pan at its base.

A second oval pit (63) was also recorded in this area, c.3.00 m long and 1.50 m wide, with fairly steep sides c.75 cms deep. It has already been noted that the two lower layers (97 and 141: fig.16,A-B) may on chronological grounds be regarded as a separate feature (161) belonging to the earliest phase of Roman activity, which could then have remained in use throughout the subsequent period. The base of the presumably later pit (63) was sealed by a layer of very mixed multi-coloured puddled clays (65:fig.16,A-B) exactly similar to the basal layer of the other oval pit (46) associated with this phase. The remaining fill was composed of a layer of soft grey clayey silt mixed with small pebbles (64:fig.16,A-B) c.45 cms thick, and consistent with the upper fills of the other two pits already described above.

A large shallow rectangular feature (21) ran under the western edge of the excavated area and measured c.3.70 by 2.20 m with long gently shelving sides c.50 cms deep. The lower fill comprised a layer of hard and compact black/dark red brown concretion, mixed with iron staining (20:fig.15,A-B), underlying the upper fill of coarse grey silt mixed with small pebbles and some larger cobbles (33). It is possible that the actual cut of this feature was represented by the junction of contexts 20 and 33, and that context 20 may simply have been the resultant product on the old ground surface of whatever activity was undertaken in the pit.

Two short lengths of gully may also be ascribed to this

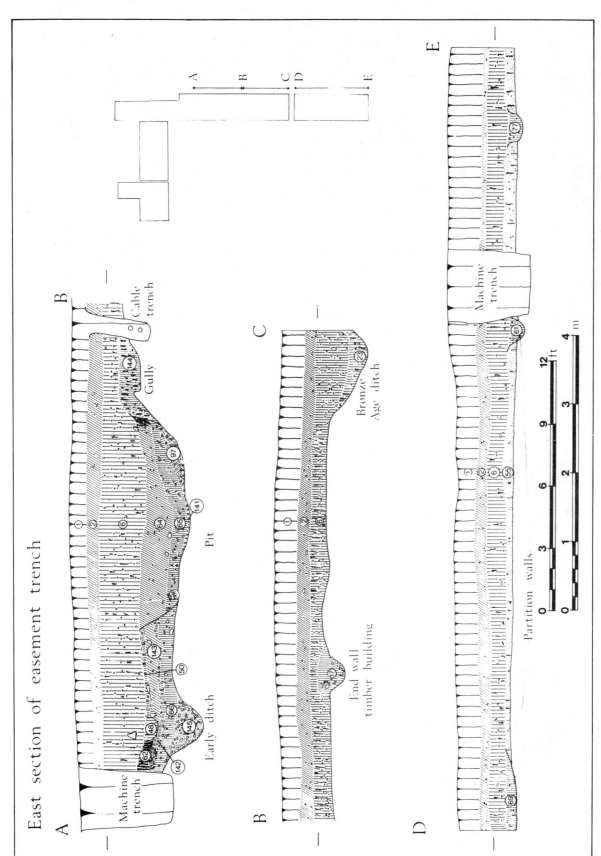

East section of easement trench

Fig.16.

phase of activity. The first (138) ran from the eastern edge of the excavated area adjacent to pit 63 in a south-westerly direction for 1.20 m before terminating in a butt end next to pit 46. This gully was 70 cms wide, with steep sides and a flat bottom 12 cms deep. The fill (144) was a uniform grey clayey silt mixed with iron pan (fig.16,A-B). The second gully, c.40 cms wide and 20 cms deep, with a slightly flattened bottom, also ran from the eastern edge of the excavated area, north of pit 63, for c.1.00 m before coming to a butt end. The fill (48) was composed of a uniform dark grey/black clayey silt. The exact association of these two short lengths of gully with the pits was unclear. However, it is possible that they may have formed a partial boundary to this area.

The features associated with this phase were all generally isolated from one another stratigraphically. Nevertheless, the general conformity and similarity of the pit fills indicates that they were at least broadly contemporary. It also seems likely that the lower fills of all these pits may have resulted from the activities associated with their use, whilst the upper fills represent either a gradual silting or deliberate infilling, after the features had fallen into disuse. There were no firm indications regarding the function or purpose of these pits. However, the presence of small quantities of metal working residues in one (63) may point to some industrial activity; in addition, the pit fills also contained some domestic debris. The large oval pit (46) produced a sizeable group of coarse pottery (nos.304-308, 310-311) and samian (nos.54-55) which included very little residual material, and is mainly later Antonine in date, and a second pit also produced a piece of mortarium of similar date (no.309). The horizon which sealed most of these features (43:fig.18,F-G) produced a group of coarse pottery (nos.312-318) and samian (nos.56-58) broadly contemporary with the material recovered from the pits, and indicates that, in this area, there was no long hiatus between the excavation and use of the pits and gullies and the deposition of horizon 43.

The Defences. (Figs.17-18).
a) Pre-defence features (Period 2).
In addition to the pit (160) and ditch (134) already described, two other features, presumably a pair of construction trenches, also certainly predated the defences. Both were discovered at a late stage during the excavations, on the northernmost fringe of the excavated area, and ran into that part of the site that originally appeared to contain no trace of Roman activity. It was not, therefore, possible to investigate more than a short length of either feature.

The western trench (119) was c.80 cms wide and 50 cms deep, with steep sides and a flat bottom c.25 cms wide, filled by a uniform grey clayey silt (118. fig.18,E-A). The second trench (114) ran parallel to 119, and was c.90 cms wide and 50 cms deep with a U-shaped profile having gently sloping sides. A primary silt of clean beige clay (152. fig.18,E-A) lined the bottom and sides of the

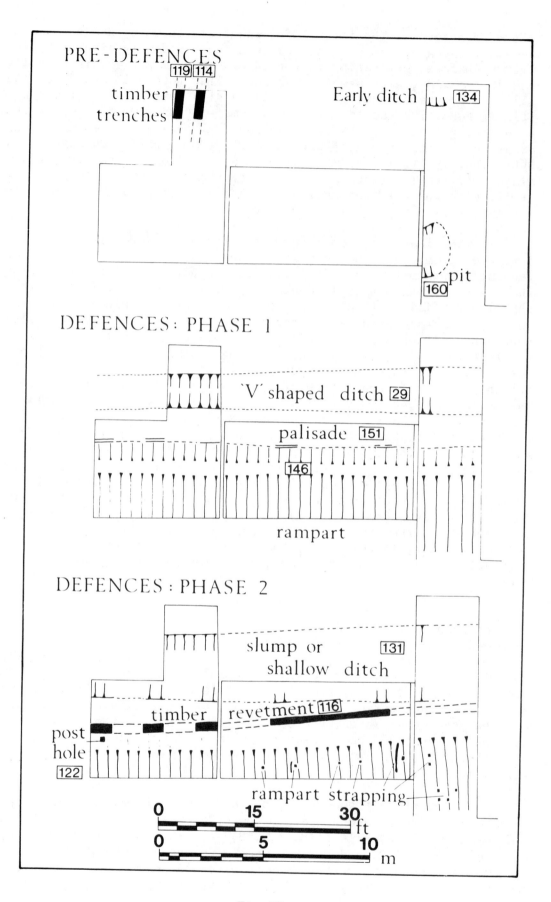

PRE-DEFENCES

timber trenches [119] [114]

Early ditch [134]

pit [160]

DEFENCES: PHASE 1

'V' shaped ditch [29]

palisade [151]

[146]

rampart

DEFENCES: PHASE 2

slump or shallow ditch [131]

timber revetment [116]

post hole [122]

rampart strapping

0   15   30 ft
0   5   10 m

Fig.17.

trench, whilst the main fill (115) was a uniform brown/grey silt (fig.18,E-A). The two trenches were only 10 cms apart.

Both features were entirely cut away by the later U-shaped ditch, and did not continue beyond the southern edge of that ditch underneath the rampart. The section across the two trenches (fig.18,E-A) demonstrates that 119 appears to have been cut later than 114. It was possible to excavate one small exploratory trench by machine 5 m north of the excavated area, in order to investigate these features further. The earlier eastern trench (114) appeared to turn through 90 degrees eastwards, whilst the western trench (119) continued to run north, getting gradually more shallow until it disappeared.

These features presumably represent construction trenches for timber sill beams, and must, therefore, indicate the presence of structures in this area. A watching brief conducted during the construction of the sheltered housing provided no further information regarding either these features or any other evidence of Roman activity in this area. Nevertheless, it should be noted that the gradual shallowing of the western trench (119) may indicate that the absence of Roman features was the product of post-Roman erosion, rather than the absence of Roman activity. The very small volume of coarse pottery recovered from these features includes a beaker dated c.A.D.80-130 (320) as well as a later Black-burnished jar perhaps derived from disturbance during construction of the defences (321).

b) First Phase Defences (Period 3).

An east-west line of defensive works was recorded at the northern end of the excavated area. The earliest phase comprised a rampart and palisade fronted by a berm and V-shaped ditch. The rampart appears to have been rebuilt during a later refurbishment of the defences, and it was, therefore, difficult to distinguish which layers of make up belonged to the earlier or later phase of rampart construction, and, in places, the earlier rampart hardly seems to have survived. Where definitely identifiable, the earlier rampart (146) was represented by a compact layer of grey brown silt mixed with iron pan (fig.18,F-G) c.20 cms thick, together with a compact layer of grey sandy clay mixed with small pebbles (162) c.25 cms thick, and a very hard dark red-brown deposit mixed with iron pan (28: fig.18, C-D). Running along the northern edge of this rampart was a small trench (151), c.50 cms deep, and originally c.50 cms wide. with steep sides, and a V-shaped profile (fig.18,C-D), presumably for a palisade, or revetment. This 'palisade' formed the front face of the earlier rampart. The earlier rampart had no internal structures, and it seems likely, therefore, that it may have been of dumped construction and fronted fronted by a slight, wooden fence.

A berm c.1.50 m wide separated the rampart and palisade from the steep sided V-shaped ditch (29), which was c.1.00 m deep and originally would have been c.1.90 m wide. At some time between the establishment of this defensive system and its later refurbishment, the southern edge of the ditch and the berm were cut away by a shallow flat-bottomed shelf (133) c.1,50 m wide. This event certainly occurred before the palisade either collapsed or was removed and the rampart fell into disrepair. It must also have taken place soon after the V-shaped ditch was dug, as the primary clean grey silt within the shelf (110:fig.18,A-B,C-D,F-G) was contiguous with both the primary silt of the V-shaped ditch (fig.18,A-B,F-G) and the palisade trench (fig.18,C-D). The upper fill of this shelf comprised a layer of grey/beige clayey silt mixed with small pebbles (154:fig.18,F-G). In one part of the ditch some material was apparently deposited before any silting could have occurred (155, 156 and 157: fig.18,F-G). It is possible that this may represent the deliberate infilling of the ditch to a level consistent with the base of the shelf described above, effectively replacing the berm and V-shaped ditch with a shallower but broader ditch immediately fronting the rampart and palisade.

There seems to have been no apparent motive for this remodelling of the defences so soon after their construction as it did not make them a greater obstacle. This first phase of defences produced only a small quantity of datable coarse pottery (nos.322-325) and no samian, but appears to have been constructed in the late Antonine period or later.

In parts of the easement trench south of the phase 1 defences, the (industrial?) pits and gullies were superseded by a horizon of coarse grey silt of varying thickness (6:fig.16,A-E, and fig.18,F-G) and this layer also produced mainly later Antonine material (coarse pottery: nos.312-318, samian: nos.56-58). The exact relationship between this horizon and the first phase of defences (fig.18,F-G) was obscured by their later remodelling. Consequently the sequence of occupation and land use represented in this part of the extra-mural settlement by the later series of pits, the primary defences, and the general horizon described above, is unclear. All these features have produced mainly late Antonine material and may, therefore, be seen as broadly contemporary in date. Nevertheless, it was apparent from the general silting observed in the V-shaped ditch, the shelf and the palisade trench, that the phase 1 defences fell into disrepair fairly soon after their establishment; the horizon, context 6, overlying the pits, also indicates that there was a hiatus in the occupation of the vicus at this location at approximately the same time as the primary defences began to decay, although whether these defences were actually contemporary with the use of the pits, remains unclear.

c) Second Phase Defences (Period 4).
The second phase of defences is represented by a refurbished rampart, with a timber revetment, fronted by a fairly shallow ditch-like feature. The rampart (147) was c.4.80 m wide and ran on a slightly different alignment to its precursor (fig.17), and consisted of a basal layer (153) composed of compact grey brown silt mixed with iron pan (fig.18,F-G), surmounted by the main body of rampart make-up. The rampart proper was composed of two parallel cores of hard concreted material which varied from a very hard black/dark red brown deposit mixed with iron pan (92:fig.18,F-G) to

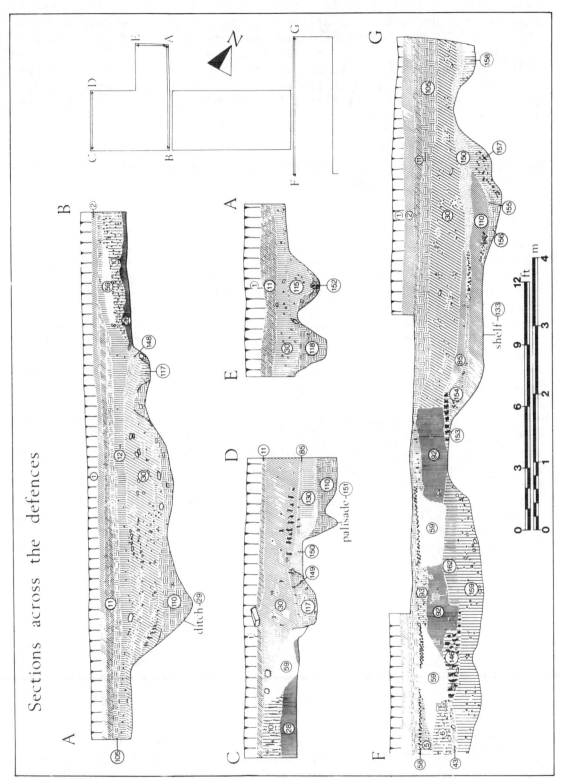

Sections across the defences

Fig.18.

a compact grey black silt mixed with iron pan and small pebbles (93:fig.18,F-G and 10:fig.18,C-D,A-B). The third major component of this rampart consisted of two substantial deposits of soft white clay (59) running parallel to one another along its length representing decayed turf. At the western end of the excavated area, this turf deposit certainly lined the forward edge of the rampart (fig.18,A-B,C-D), however, to the east the rampart was wider, and this band of clay ran into the centre of the rampart body at that point (fig.18,F-G). Also at the eastern end of the excavated area, a second deposit of white clay was observed, apparently lining the rear face of the rampart.

The body of the later rampart contained traces of both vertical and horizontal timber strapping (fig.17) indicating a boxed construction. The forward edge of the rampart was faced by a large revetment trench (116) c.80 cms wide and 40 cms deep, with a U-shaped profile and a grey brown clayey silt fill (117 and 149,fig.18,A-B,C-D). This feature, therefore, represents the construction trench for a substantial timber wall facing the rampart, and its alignment is also echoed by the line of vertical strapping posts referred to above. A large stone packed post pit (122) was observed close to the western edge of the excavated area, behind the revetment trench (fig.17). The presence of this feature certainly suggests a major timber structure above the rampart, however, no other elements of such a structure were present within the excavated area, and consequently, although it is tempting to interpret this post as indicating a tower, such observations remain speculative. It may actually post-date the rampart.

No substantial ditch was observed in association with the refurbished rampart, although one may be located beyond the limit of excavation. It was apparent, however, that the rampart was fronted by a fairly large depression (131) c.4.00 m wide and only 70 cms deep, slumped over the original V-shaped ditch and shelf (fig.18,A-B,12,30,148; C-D,30,85,130; E-A,30; F-G,30,85,150). Whilst the depression over the original ditch does not contribute to the effectiveness of the defensive works, it would certainly have increased the height of the rampart a little. Very little datable material was recovered from the refurbished defences. The coarse pottery (nos.326-330) and samian (no.59) from the rampart and the fill of the slump includes earlier material as well as that dated to the later second century A.D. However, this feature was deliberately infilled, and the material, therefore, presumably derived from elsewhere in the vicinity, and consequently the possiblility of residuality and contamination cannot be ignored. The presence of a possible radiate coin dating to c.A.D.270 (no.684) perhaps indicates that the later phase of defences should be dated to some time late in the third century A.D.

The tail of the later rampart overlay the general horizon (6) described above, and it is possible that this layer, which contained mainly later Antonine material (presumably residual) may represent a deliberate clearing and levelling of the area of industrial activity, rather than a gradual process of decay. The clearance of the area and the preparation of the ground surface may consequently have been an integral part of the remodelling of the defences, and have occurred immediately prior to the construction of the later rampart. The absence of any occupation associated with this horizon suggests that the area remained an open space throughout the life of those defences.

Period 5. Levelling and Sealing of the Defences.

It is clear from the sections across the fill of the depression fronting the refurbished rampart, that this feature was deliberately filled. In places, tip lines were recorded (fig.18,A-B). In addition, the main fill of the revetment trench was entirely consistent with the fill of the depression (30), and was overlain at this point by a thin horizon (148) within the general fill of the depression. The rampart revetment did not, therefore, decay **in situ**, but rather must have been deliberately uprooted, and then filled in and levelled at the same time as the depression.

Several main elements in the fill of the depression were observed during the course of excavation. A band of orange yellow sandy silt (150:fig.18,C-D,F-G) presumably represents the disturbed and redeposited natural subsoil, associated with the cutting of the depression rather than its deliberate infilling. The basal fill comprised a light coloured clayey silt (85 and 130:fig.18,C-D,F-G), which underlay the main fill (30) formed by a generally grey clayey silt mixed with small pebbles (fig.18,A-B,C-D,E-A,F-G). The upper fill of the depression (12) was only observed with confidence in one section (fig.18,A-B), where it formed an horizon of light grey clayey silt. At this point, however, this layer continued across the top of the surviving rampart. It seems likely, therefore, that prior to the deposition of this horizon, the rampart had been deliberately levelled.

The entire width of both the levelled rampart and the infilled depression was overlain by narrow bands of yellow and grey clay (11 and 105:fig.18,A-B,C-D,E-A,F-G). These horizons, were probably derived from the rampart itself and certainly extended some distance to the north. They sealed the slighted defences and to the south of the rampart, they corresponded to the narrow horizon (5) which represents the latest Roman activity occurring in the remainder of the easement trench. These upper levels produced very little material. However, scraps of later coarse pottery (nos.331-335) do indicate some activity in the area during the first half of the fourth century A.D. No sherds of Crambeck Ware, ubiquitous in the region from c.A.D.367 onwards, were recovered, and it must be assumed that, by this time, all Roman activity in the vicinity had effectively ceased.

Discussion

With the exception of a fairly substantial timber structure and a number of possibly industrial pits, little evidence survived to characterise the nature of Roman occupation in this part of the civil settlement. The earliest phase of activity is likely to have been pre-Hadrianic in date, from c.A.D.70/80 and terminating by c.A.D.120. The building, possibly deliberately demolished in the post-Hadrianic period, may have been contemporary with some of these earlier pits, and was certainly succeeded by a second phase of pits (set within plot boundaries?), dated mainly to the later Antonine period. The function of these features is not clear. However, the presence of large, fairly open areas within extra-mural and other minor settlements is well documented, both in Ribchester (Ch.3 and Ch.6), and elsewhere (Todd 1970, p.119; Birley 1973, p.33). Little is known regarding the tenurial patterns within such settlements and their relationship with agricultural activity in their immediate environs (Casey 1981, p.126; Jones 1984, p.84), and at Ribchester details of layout are not yet apparent. This building (of indeterminate function) together with the (industrial?) pits may have been dependent on, and lie to the rear of, strip housing alongside the north road running out of the fort, identified nearby in 1973.

Faint traces of structures recorded along the northern edge of the excavated area suggest that earlier occupation here may have been more extensive than originally anticipated, although much of the evidence appears to have been destroyed by post-Roman activity. During the later Antonine period or later, an insubstantial rampart and ditch were constructed north of the contemporary industrial activity, and then almost immediately modified and remodelled. A more imposing rampart but a shallower ditch were reconstructed on approximately the same alignment, possibly during the latter half of the third century, although no evidence of any contemporary occupation survived within the excavated area. The defences were finally demolished and levelled at some point within the fourth century A.D.

Unfortunately, the quantity of well dated material recovered during the course of excavation was extremely limited. Only a small number of contexts were either sealed or firmly stratified, and few of those contained any adequate dating evidence. Consequently, the dates ascribed to the main phases of activity should be regarded as general indications only.

In particular, the dating evidence from both of the phases of defences is especially poor, and consisted of a small volume of samian and coarse wares, mainly from the fill of the ditches, as well as a single poorly preserved coin (no.684). The importance of accurately dating earthwork defences, together with the problems involved, has recently been discussed in detail by Frere (1984, p.64) and Crickmore (1984, pp.32-46). Both emphasise the unreliability of dates derived from material from ditch fills, as well as the possible residual nature of material recovered from the body of ramparts (which only provides a **terminus post quem** that may not relate closely to a date of construction.

The limited area excavated and the nature of the evidence

recorded, preclude any detailed conclusions, and the problems of interpretation are further compounded by the general lack of adequately dated material. The presence of defences around at least part of the extra-mural settlement at Ribchester is clearly of some importance, with implications not only for our interpretation of the nature and function of the Roman settlement at Ribchester itself, but also for our understanding of the development, status and role of all such civil settlements in the North. These issues are addressed in more detail below (see Chapter 9).

CONTEXT CATALOGUE.

Date of periods

Period 1	Bronze Age Cremations
Period 2	Late first century A.D. – Hadrianic
Period 3	Later Antonine
Period 4	Third century A.D.
Period 5	First half of the fourth century A.D.

Context Category		Period
1.	Topsoil.	
2.	Disturbed ploughsoil.	
3.	Fill of modern cable trench (4).	
4.	Cable trench.	
5.	Horizon: level contemporary with slighting of defences.	5
6.	Horizon: level immediately preceding later defences: material presumably residual.	3/4
7.	Part of 6	3/4
8.	Natural subsoil.	
9.	Natural subsoil.	
10.	Part of core of later rampart (147).	4
11.	Redeposited natural clay, sealing defences.	5
12.	Upper fill of depression (131) fronting later rampart (147).	5
13.	Fill of foundation trench (14).	2
14.	N-S foundation trench of building (163).	2
15.	Natural subsoil.	
16.	Natural subsoil.	
17.	Fill of foundation trench (18).	2
18.	Foundation trench of N end wall of building (163).	2
19.	Natural subsoil.	
20.	Lower fill of pit (21).	3
21.	Shallow rectangular pit.	3
22.	Disturbed and redeposited natural subsoil.	2
23.	Fill of ditch (24)	1
24.	Bronze Age ditch enclosing cremations.	1
25.	Upper fill of pit (38).	3
26.	Fill of small (?) pit.	1-3?
27.	Small pit/depression in natural subsoil.	1-3?
28.	Part of early rampart (146).	3

Context	Category	Period
29.	V-shaped ditch fronting early rampart (146).	3
30.	Fill of depression (131) fronting later rampart (147).	4/5
31.	Post construction pit: part of building (163).	2
32.	Upper fill of post construction pit(31).	2
33.	Upper fill of pit (21).	3
34.	Possible true cut of pit (21).	3
35.	Post-pipe within post construction pit (31).	2
36.	Part of post post construction pit (31).	2
37.	Upper fill of pit (46).	3
38.	Circular pit.	3
39.	Fill of post construction pit	2
40.	Part of pit (46).	3
41.	Layer of fill within pit (46).	3
42.	Part of horizon (6).	3/4
43.	Part of horizon (6).	3/4
44.	Layer of fill within pit (46).	3
45.	Basal layer of pit (46).	3
46.	Large oval pit.	3
47.	Part of horizon (6).	3/4
48.	Upper fill of small gully (49)	3
49.	Small gully.	3
50.	Horizon: ground surface associated with earlier pits?	2/3?
51.	Part of horizon (50).	3
52.	Fill of shallow depression (53) in surface of pit (63), upper fill of pit?	3/4
53.	Irregular depression.	3/4
54.	Cremation burial.	1
55.	Disturbed natural ground surface.	1
56.	Cremation burial.	1
57.	Cremation burial.	1
58.	Pebble surface over slighted rampart.	5
59.	Decayed turf stack (?) part of later rampart (147).	4
60.	E-W partition of building (163).	2
61.	Fill of shallow trench (60) – partition?	2
62.	Continuous with horizon (50).	2/3?
63.	Large oval pit.	3
64.	Fill of pit (63).	3
65.	Lower fill of pit (63).	3
66.	Horizon: possibly contemporary with early pits.	2?
67.	Cremation burial.	1
68.	Cremation burial.	1
69.	Fill of gully (70) – partition.	2
70.	E-W partion of building (163).	2
71.	Fill of shallow circular pit (73).	2?
72.	Part of disturbed ground surface (55).	1
73.	Circular pit: part of building (163)?	2?
74.	Post construction pit: part of building (163).	2
75.	Fill of post construction pit (74).	2

Context	Category	Period
76.	Internal partition of building (163)?	2
77.	Fill of gully (76) – partition.	2
78.	Fill of circular feature.	
79.	Shallow circular feature: indeterminate.	
80.	Fill of ?post construction pit (81).	2?
81.	Possible post construction pit of building (163).	2?
82.	Fill of post construction pit (83).	2
83.	Post construction pit: part of building (163).	2
84.	Part of horizon (11).	5
85.	Lower fill of depression (131) fronting later rampart (147)	4/5
86.	Part of later rampart (147).	4
87.	Part of later rampart (147).	4
88.	Part of later rampart (147).	4
89.	Part of later rampart (147).	4
90.	Part of later rampart (147).	4
91.	Part of later rampart (147).	4
92.	Part of early rampart (146).	3
93.	Part of later rampart (147).	4
94.	Fill of early pit (95).	2
95.	Irregular early pit.	2
96.	Early ditch.	2
97.	Fill of (?early) pit 161.	2?
98.	Fill of pit (99).	2
99.	Sub-rectangular pit, ?hearth.	2
100.	Fill of ?hearth (104).	4/5
101.	Post construction pit: part of building (163).	2
102.	Fill of post construction pit (101).	2
103.	Post construction pit: ?part of building (163).	2
104.	?Hearth in surface of slighted rampart (147).	5
105.	Part of horizon (11).	5
106.	Post construction pit: part of building (163).	2
107.	Fill of post construction pit (106).	2
108.	Post construction pit: part of building (163).	2
109.	Fill of post construction pit (108).	2
110.	Primary silt within ditch (29), shelf (133) and palisade trench (151) of early defences.	3
111.	True extent of ?hearth (99).	2
112.	Lowest fill of ?hearth (99/111).	2
113.	?Decayed turf stack: part of rampart (147).	4
114.	Foundation trench for timber building.	2
115.	Fill of foundation trench (114).	2
116.	Foundation trench for timber revetment to later rampart (147).	4
117.	Fill of foundation trench (116).	4
118.	Fill of foundation trench (119).	2
119.	Foundation trench for timber building.	2
120.	Fill of linear feature (121).	4
121.	Decayed horizontal timber strapping within later rampart (147).	4
122.	Post construction pit in later rampart (147).	4/5
123.	Fill of post construction pit (122).	4/5

Context	Category	Period
124.	Stone packing of post construction pit (122).	4/5
125.	Post-pipe within post construction pit (122).	4/5
126.	Fill of linear feature (127).	4
127.	Horizontal strapping of later rampart (147).	4
128.	Part of fill (30) of depression (131).	4/5
129.	Layer of fill of ditch (29).	3
130.	Layer of fill of depression (131).	4/5
131.	Depression fronting later rampart (147).	4
132.	Layer of fill of shelf (133).	3
133.	Shelf: modifying S edge of ditch (29).	3
134.	Early (?) ditch.	2?
135.	Part of fill of pit (159)	2
136.	Small circular pit.	2
137.	Part of floor level of building (163).	2
138.	Short length of gully .	2
139.	Primary silt at base of post-pipe (35).	2
140.	Primary silt at base of pit (38).	3
141.	Basal layer of pit (161).	2?
142.	Horizon: ?ground surface, associated with earlier pits?	2
143.	Horizon: build up prior to excavation of later pits.	2/3?
144.	Fill of gully (138).	2
145.	Fill of ditch (96).	2
146.	Early rampart.	3
147.	Later rampart.	4
148.	Layer of fill of depression (131).	4/5
149.	Upper fill of foundation trench (116).	4
150.	Disturbed natural subsoil redeposited after construction of later defences.	4
151.	Palisade trench.	3
152.	Primary silt of foundation trench (114).	2
153.	Part of rampart (146/147).	3/4
154.	Upper fill of shelf (133).	3/4
155.	Layer of fill of dich (29).	3
156.	Primary silt of ditch (29).	3
157.	Part of fill of ditch (29).	3
158.	Fill of ditch (134).	2?
159.	Fill of pit (160).	2
160.	Pit below rampart (146).	2
161.	Surviving portion of (early?) pit.	2?
162.	Part of early rampart (146).	3
163.	Rectangular timber building in S of easement trench.	2

Chapter 5
TRIAL EXCAVATIONS IN THE PLAYING FIELDS CAR PARK, 1973.
By B.J.N.Edwards & P.V.Webster.

Plans by Preston RDC to convert the two small fields between the rear of Parsonage Avenue and the access road to the Playing Fields into a car park occasioned trial work in 1973. Excavation for the Department of the Environment was directed by the authors and Mrs J.Webster with the help of the Ribble Archaeological Society.

Excavation was largely by machine-cut section, designed to test the area for Roman buildings and with two particular problems in mind. The first of these concerned the antiquity of the lane surrounding the Playing Fields. This has a configuration not unlike that of a Roman fort and has given rise to speculation that it may mask a Roman military structure, perhaps an early temporary camp. The lane bends slightly, almost opposite the present field gate into the Playing Fields and, at the time of excavation, a depression continued the line of the lane across the area to be occupied by the car park. If the lane did, indeed, mark the line of an earlier structure, then a section across the depression should have revealed its nature. A mechanical slot (Slot A) was, therefore, cut about 5 metres west of the eastern boundary of the plot (see plan, fig.19). The cut showed a considerable depth of ploughsoil (40-60 cms, 16-24 inches) and that the depression was an entirely surface phenomenon. Perhaps it had been caused by traffic along an old field boundary. If so, then we can assume that the course of both the depression and the lane are dictated by the post-Roman field system rather than by anything more ancient.

Beneath the ploughsoil in slot A was between 10 and 40 cms of mixed grey clay and gravel, probably resulting from the ploughing of the subsoil. One patch of humus and burnt daub was observed between 2.75 and 4.25m (9 - 13.5ft.) north of the boundary of the lane. This feature was apparently derived from the destruction of a nearby timber building and Roman pottery from the vicinity provides a possible date. The slot did, however, yield a quantity of post-medieval pottery and so dating is not secure. The section of this trench (RCP73A) has not been illustrated here but will be deposited in the site archive for future reference.

The second problem on which it seemed possible to shed some light was that of the line of the road leading northwards from the fort. To locate this, a slot was cut by machine c.10m south of the rear boundary of the gardens of Parsonage Avenue (cf. plan fig.19, Slot B; the section drawing will be deposited in the site archive). The section suggests that two road surfaces were located. The lowest road consisted of waterwashed sand and gravel with some charcoal forming a layer c.4.4m (14.5 ft.) wide (B.8). Either side were slight indications of buildings (burnt clay/daub, B.7, a layer containing burnt daub and charcoal, B.13 and possibly the grey clay B.6) although no definite building positions could be identified.

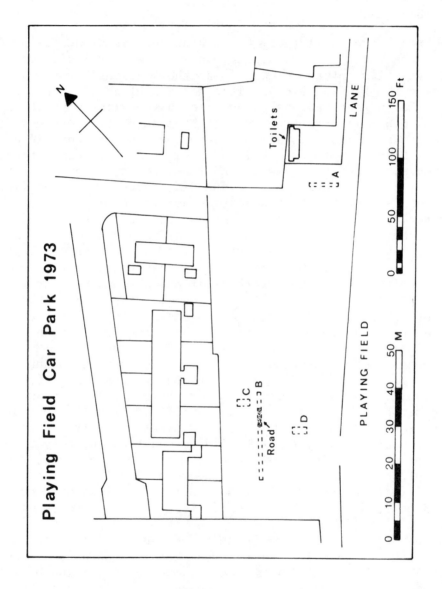

Fig.19.

Superimposed on these features was a substantial gravel dump (B.3) which marked the later road. This dump was of 0.5m (1.5 ft.) max. thickness and about 6m (19.5 ft.) wide, although some lateral spread during use seems likely, particularly as the road seems to have spread over the edge of a silted ditch (B.10-12) 2m wide and 0.5m deep which lay on its West. The ditch is presumably to be associated with the second road as it cuts the building debris, B.13, which edges the first road. Certainly the ditch went out of use before the final abandonment of the second road, not only because of the position of the spread of gravel already mentioned but also because it was sealed by a substantial level of yellow daub which itself spread over the edge of the spread road (B.9).The daub extended c.3.25m (10.5 ft.) westwards from the road edge and presumably marks the site of a structure which once fronted the road. A similar structure to the east of the road is suggested by a block of clay and stones (B.4) and a patch of buff daub (B.5) giving a structure a least 2.5m (8.5 ft.) deep and similarly overlapping the spread road surface. Both probable buildings lay immediately beneath the ploughsoil and had been extensively damaged by agricultural activity (which extended a full metre down to the natural sand at the extreme West of the section). It is probably for this same reason that the small areas excavated by hand south of Section B (plan fig.19, area D) and north of it (area C) yielded Roman pottery but otherwise added nothing of significance to the picture already revealed. Finds from B and the adjacent areas range in date from Flavian (including samian of form 29) to mid 3rd century but with a predominance of late first and early second century pieces (pottery reports will be placed in the site archive; see also Part 3, no.336).

It will be seen that the remains suggested by slot B are not extensive and this, together with the relative paucity of finds, suggests that the whole area is on the outskirts of the civil settlement at Ribchester. Ribbon development along the line of the road north from the fort had undoubtedly occured but probably only at the time of maximum activity in this part of the settlement. The area did not hold the promise of extensive remains. Nevertheless, it is pleasing to record, that as a result of the trial excavations, it was agreed that penetration below the ploughsoil would be minimised during the construction of the car park and that this much needed feature thus seals and preserves, rather than destroys, what Roman remains there are.

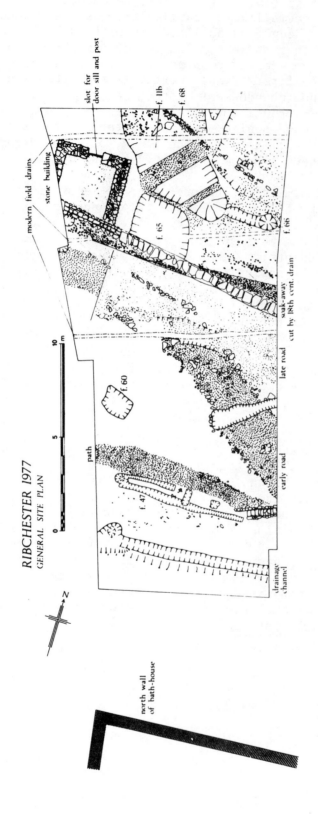

RIBCHESTER 1977
GENERAL SITE PLAN

slot for door sill and post

f. 11b

f. 68

modern field drains

store building

f. 65

f. 66

soak-away

cut by 18th cent. drain

late road

f. 60

path

f. 47

early road

drainage channel

north wall of bath-house

Fig. 20.

Chapter 6
THE ACCESS ROAD SITE, 1977
By J.H.S.Witherington

Introduction

The bath-house at Ribchester, situated some 100 metres north of the Fort, has long attracted the attention of antiquarians and archaeologists. Prior to 1976, the baths had been left open and had become overgrown. In September of that year, Ribble Valley Borough Council, in cooperation with Lancashire County Council, put forward a scheme which involved the re-excavation of the bath-house and the landscaping of the site and an area of derelict land, once an orchard, to the north (SD 6508 3520). Included in this scheme was a proposal to provide a road off Greenside (B 6245) which would serve the bath-house and provide rear access for houses on the East side of Water Street.

In this particular case, however, excavation in connection with consolidation could not be funded by the Department of the Environment from its 'rescue' budget. Construction of the access road, on the other hand, posed a threat to an area of c. 600 sq.m. in a potentially important part of the **vicus** to the north of the fort and here a rescue excavation was funded by the Department and carried out by the University of Lancaster

Excavation began on 12th June 1977 and continued for 8 weeks. The first 2 weeks of excavation were carried out with the help of extra-mural students of the Liverpool University Institute of Extension Studies, coordinated by P.J.Davey; I should like to thank him for his help and for his comments on the post-Roman pottery.

The remainder of the excavation work was done by students of the University of Lancaster and other volunteers including members of the Ribble Archaeological Society. In directing the excavation, I was assisted by R.C.Turner whose work on site and current thoughts contributed to many parts of this report; I am particularly grateful for his supervision of the planning and survey work. C.M.Reed gave me invaluable help as site assistant and the finds were processed by Helen Lockwood.

Helpful cooperation was received from many people both before and during the excavation. In particular I would like to thank the late Dorothy Charlesworth (Department of Environment), J.Stewart (Ribble Valley Borough Council Planning Department), B.J.N.Edwards for his information on the bath-house, Nancy Dixon for providing me with unpublished excavation material, A.C.H.Olivier for assistance in setting up the excavation and for advice throughout and Ian Robson for his patience over our accommodation difficulties. Many services were provided by the University of Lancaster; special thanks are due to J.Cansfield, B.Phillips and K.Turner. Dr D.C.A.Shotter of the Department of

Classics and Archaeology gave me valuable support in both academic and administrative matters. I am also very grateful to all who contributed specialist reports.

THE EXCAVATIONS (Fig.20).

Although the threatened area amounted to c.600 sq.m. it was possible to open for excavation only a little over 400 sq.m. due to a large amount of extremely loose overburden at the south end of the site (a legacy of earlier bath-house excavations), a high unsteady stone wall lining the west side of the site and recent tipping of debris over the whole area. At the northern end of the site, a stone garage, due to be demolished, in fact remained standing. Ultimately it was feasible only to cut a trench by machine alongside the garage. However, it was found found that digging of the garage foundation or of the garden to the east had already effectively removed all traces of Roman occupation.

Once the site was cleared and topsoil removed by machine, it soon became clear that the nature of the archaeological deposits was rather different from those in areas south of the bath-house, (Chapter 7 below) in other parts of the **vicus** and in the fort itself. There, excavation has often revealed deep stratigraphy with the lower layers preserving timber and other organic remains. The School foundation trenches (see Chapter 8 below) and the 1976 trenches in the north of the **vicus** (Chapter 3 above), for example, each yielded a wealth of such material. The Access Road site, however, provides a stark contrast. The stratigraphy in most places was little over 1 m. deep, much of it topsoil or recent or post-Roman disturbance and there were no well-preserved organic remains.   The structures, moreover, were few and so distributed that, in many cases, their stratigraphic relationship could not be determined. Furthermore, although sherds of nearly 2000 pots and 150 small finds were recovered, pottery groups tended not to be datable closely enough for layers or features to be distinguished chronologically by finds. Of the 16 coins, all but 4 were residual or unstratified.

For these reasons, therefore, the structures have not been 'phased'.   Each structure is described in turn starting at the north end of the site. A discussion and summary are offered at the end of each section.

Earlier excavation

A trench 6 yards long and 1 yard wide was found cutting through the east section (Fig.22, G-F, 2) revealing the early road surface and part of the debris area to the west. From hearsay, this is assumed to be the work of the Rev. Mr Stevens in 1967.

RIBCHESTER, ACCESS ROAD 1977

Stone building, plan and section

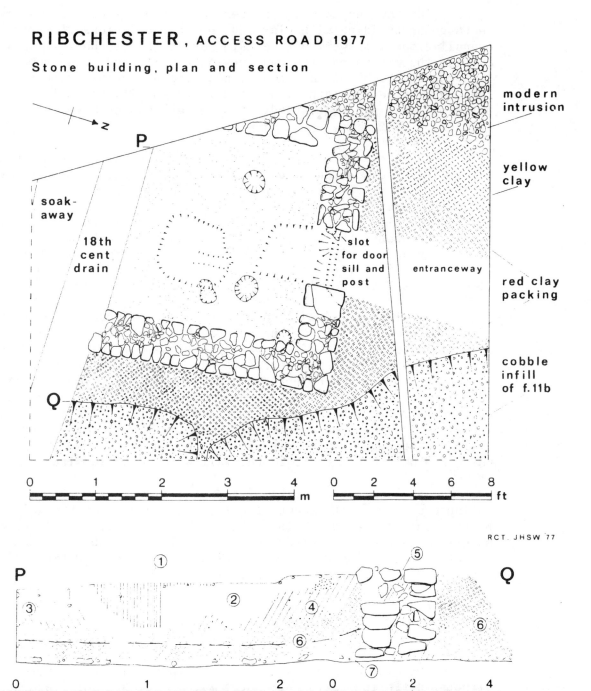

modern
intrusion

yellow
clay

red clay
packing

cobble
infill
of f.11b

soak-
away

18th
cent
drain

slot
for door
sill and
post

entranceway

RCT. JHSW 77

Fig.21.

The stone building

In the north-west corner of the site lay a small
rectangular building with clay and cobble foundations (fig.21). Its
overall dimensions were not certain as part of the west wall lay
outside the excavated area and the south wall had been removed by
the construction of a stone-lined drain, probably in the 18th
century. It had a width of 4m (13.1 ft) and if, as is likely, the
building adjoined the road, its length cannot have been much
greater.

The foundations for the floor consisted of two 10 cm.
layers of redeposited red clay (Section P-Q, 6) which were
separated by a very thin band of charcoal. The walls were 0.75m
wide, constructed of cobbles with yellow clay packing in the higher
courses (Section P-Q, 5). The lower courses, however, were heavily
buttressed around the outside of the building by a bank of red clay
0.65m high and in places over 0.5m wide. The structure, therefore,
was built with very strong, watertight foundations, apparently
almost excessively solid for a building of such a size.

The internal details are less clear. There seems to have
been only one floor in the building's history, made of rammed earth
and scattered pebbles. There were few signs of internal supports
for the roof or of any partitioning. A narrow, deep hole in the
north-east corner of the building may have had some structural
function as may the other possible post-holes shown in Fig.21. The
entrance and threshold were identified by depressions in the clay.
The slot for the door sill and hole for the door post were also
visible. Although the post itself had not survived, two iron rivets
which had helped fasten it to the wall were found **in situ.**

The occupation fill of the building was covered by a
collapse of daub. It seems likely, therefore, that the walls had
been daubed internally but whether this covered a timber
superstructure or a continuation of the clay and cobble foundations
is not certain. There were no indications as to how the building
was roofed. A tiled roof is possible, but only a small percentage
of the tiles found on the site derived from this corner and it is,
therefore, more likely that the building had a roof of timber or
thatch. It may also be worth noting that none of the window glass
came from this part of the site.

There were no signs that the building had been altered and,
although different fills were noted within it, so many fragments of
pottery and glass joined with others in different layers that the
occupation seems to have comprised but one phase. A full list of
finds will be found in the site archive. Many of the pottery
vessels are illustrated below (samian nos. 60-72, coarse pottery
nos. 341-393).

The date of the building's construction cannot be fixed
with certainty. A fragment of 'poppyhead' beaker (Gillam 1970, nos.

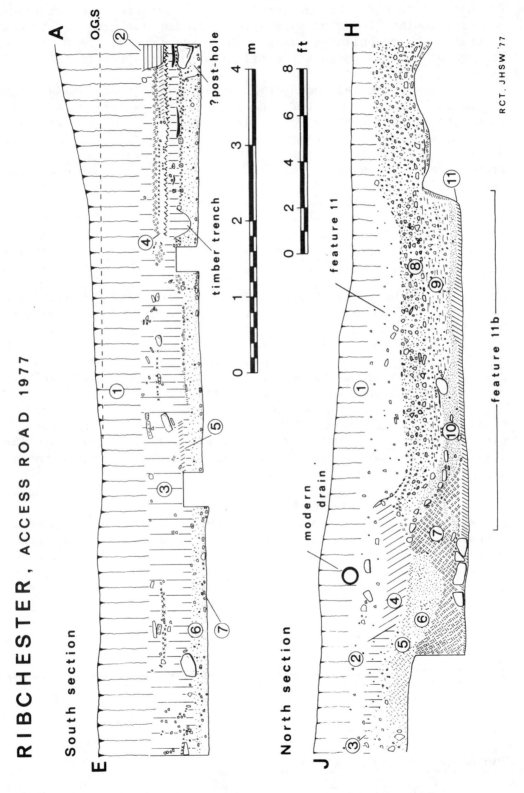

RIBCHESTER, ACCESS ROAD 1977

Fig. 22.

RCT. JHSW '77

70 & 71, A.D. 120–200) found below the foundation provides a **terminus post quem** in the Hadrianic period. The earliest occupation layers contain residual pieces of Flavian and Flavian-Trajanic date and the proportion of Hadrianic and Hadrianic-Antonine samian to sherds assigned to the Antonine period would suggest that the building was probably constructed c.A.D. 130–140. The coarse pottery would not conflict with this proposition.

The principal occupation deposit (2) contains a higher proportion of coarse pottery dating to the mid–late 2nd century than the lower layers. The samian too is almost exclusively Antonine with only one possibly residual piece. The top layers, however, contain rather more residual sherds (33%) but again are predominantly Antonine. The end of occupation in the building is marked by a collapse of daub, the latest piece in which is later 2nd century or early 3rd century. Although layer 2 contained 6 coarse pottery sherds which could be as late as the early 3rd century (see pottery nos. 263–283) there were no late samian forms (e.g. Drag. 45). The weight of evidence, therefore, favours a closing date c.A.D. 180–190 rather than two or three decades later.

The function of the building can only be guessed and the finds offer little positive help. Epigraphic evidence points to the probable existence in the Ribchester **vicus** of temples to Jupiter Dolichenos (RIB 587) and Apollo Maponus (RIB 583) but both belong to the 3rd century. The building may have been a roadside shrine but nothing amongst the finds suggests a religious or votive function and no ambulatory or precinct was found. Rectangular buildings of this size are sometimes found to be mausolea (Collingwood & Richmond 1969, 171–2) but there was no trace of a pit or chanmber. The very strong foundations may have been demanded by the height of the building, but it is hard to conceive a purpose for a tower in such a location.

The consideration of further possibilities is hampered by the absence of the south wall where there may have been another entrance fronting the road, a feature more likely in the case of such a building as a shop or tavern. The number of vessels found amounts to well over 200 and they form a fairly typical domestic assemblage with most vessel classes represented. There were also vessels of glass and shale (to be published in a later volume in this series). It is difficult, however, to imagine more than one or two people at a time living in this small building and there was no obvious hearth, little bone and few domestic items. Taking into account the lead sealing also found, it is possible that the building may have housed, on a part-time basis for fifty years or so, a person or persons with an official function related to traffic along the road to and from the bath-house.

The north-west corner of the site.

North of the stone building, the approach to its entrance was clearly visible as a shallow depression in the red clay

RIBCHESTER, ACCESS ROAD 1977

East section

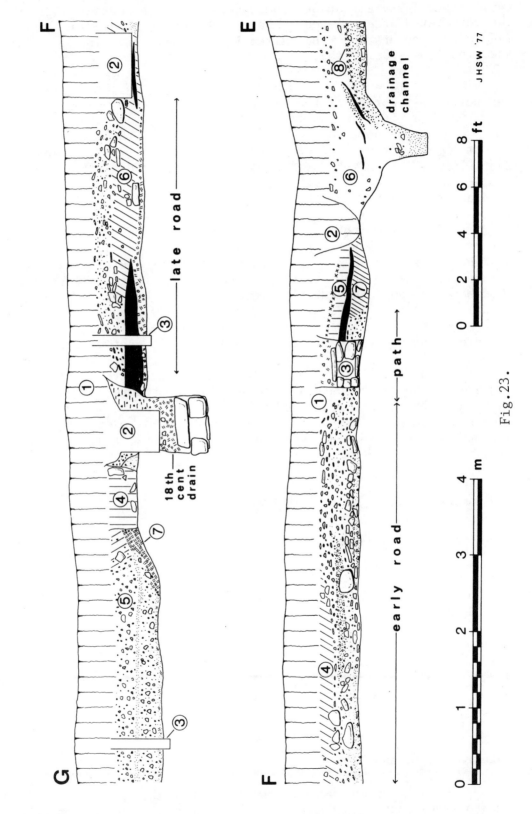

Fig. 23.

packing. To the west of the packing was an area of yellow clay
(Section J-H, 5, Fig.22) over which had accumulated a mixed layer
of daub (3) cut by a further feature containing yellow-brown clay
(4). These features can only be understood in a context wider than
the excavated area allowed. The coarse pottery (nos.374-6) is mid
2nd to 3rd century and the samian is Hadrianic-Antonine (no.74) or
Antonine (nos. 73S, 75-6).

The north-east corner of the site.

The area north of the road and east of the stone building
(about 50 sq.m.) was covered with layers of cobble to a depth of
over 0.6m. (Section G-F, 5, Fig.23). At no point did they form a
compacted surface but were loosely deposited, mixed with yellow
sand and silt. Set into the cobbles was a line of stones about
40-50 cms. wide running in an east-west direction (feature 68).
This may have been the footing for a wall, perhaps marking a
boundary. On the north side of the feature (see Fig.20) were two
post-holes set in cobble. Again, these features related to
structures outside the excavated area. The cobbles yielded nearly
400 sherds of amphorae (mainly Dressel 20). Other finds included a
denarius of Antoninus Pius (no.698, A.D.151-2), a worn sestertius
of Trajan (no.691, A.D.103-111), a small bronze flask and pottery
of mainly 2nd century date (samian nos. 77S-81; coarse pottery nos.
397-423; a full list of finds appears in the site archive). Sherds
of Antonine date were found in the lowest layers of cobble
immediately above the natural clay and it, therefore, seems likely
that the cobbles were deposited at a similar date to that of the
construction of the stone building in order to level off the pits
and other intrusions in this area (see below, features 65, 66,
11b).

Feature 11 (Figs.20, 22).

Into the top of the cobbles was cut a large flat-bottomed
intrusion (Section J-H, 11) which may simply represent a slump into
feature 11b as its limits followed much the same line. Its
dimensions were approximately 5 m. square with a depth of 60 cms.
It contained samian of Antonine date with coarse pottery of 2nd and
3rd century date, the latest piece of which was a colour coated
beaker (Gillam 1970, type 51) dating to the second half of the
third century. The 3rd century dates of three of the coarse ware
pieces suggest that this was one of the latest features on the
site. It also yielded an intaglio, a bronze cruciform fitting and
a tiny turquoise bead (to be published in a later volume in this
series).

Features 65, 66 and 11b.

The cobbles in the north-east corner of the site were laid
down to level a shallow depression, two large pits (features 65 and

RIBCHESTER, ACCESS ROAD 1977

Sections, feature 11b

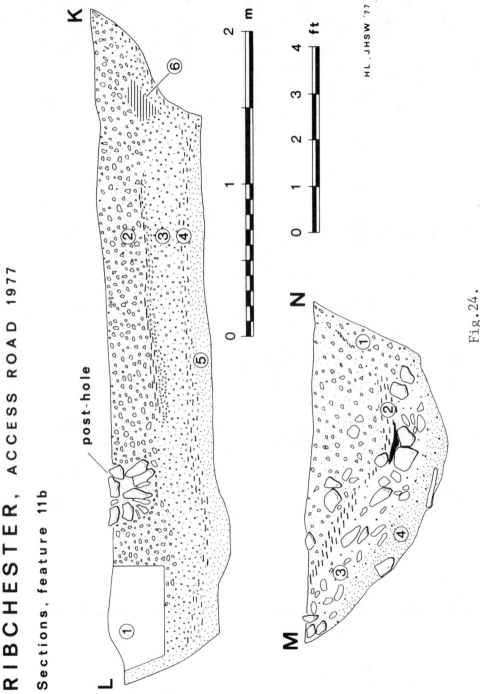

post-hole

HL.JHSW '77

Fig.24.

RIBCHESTER, ACCESS ROAD 1977

Road sections

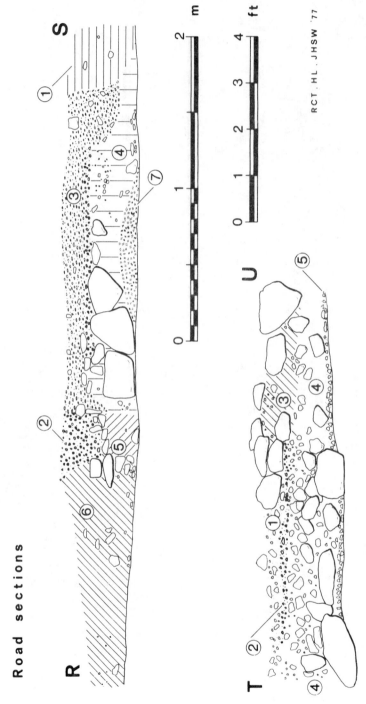

Fig. 25.

11b) and a trench-like feature with a deep hole at one end (feature 66). The largest pit was 11b (Fig.22, sections J-H and Fig.24, L-K and M-N) with a width of nearly 5m. and an excavated length of 6m. Its depth for much of its length was c. 70cms. However, towards the butt-end this increased to 90cms. The sections show a flat-bottomed profile with sides angled at about 60 degrees and a fill of silt, sand and cobbles. The contents of the smaller pit (65) were very similar but its size is uncertain as its south side was cut by the 18th century drain. Running into 11b was a trench 60cms. wide and 30cms. deep (feature 66) with a hole at the east end 80cms. in diameter and 1m. deep.

No finds came from 66, but finds from the pits are illustrated below (samian nos. 82S-83S; coarse pottery nos. 424-31) and a fuller list will be found in the site archive. Feature 11b, 10 also yielded a bronze object and a worn As of Domitian (no. 687 below). The dates of the finds, the similarity of the fills and the fact that sherds of the same vessel were found in each pit would suggest that the filling of the two features was contemporary, perhaps in the late Hadrianic-early Antonine period. When and why they were cut is a matter of conjecture but it is worth remembering that the western edge of red clay in both fetures is not natural but redeposited – the buttress of the stone building. A considerable amount of clay would have been required for the foundations of this building and these pits could have been the result of digging for it. Whatever their purpose, they were allowed to remain open long enough for silt and sand to accumulate on the bottom and sides before being filled in and levelled off to provide a large cobbled area.

The early road.

Running in an east-west direction across the site and swinging southwards towards the bath-house was a road. It was constructed with a good surface of rammed pebbles over a rubble make-up and had, at various times, been resurfaced. For part of its length, along the curve, some larger stones formed the surface, perhaps a substitute for formal kerbing (Fig.25, section T-U). The road had a width of 2.5m. (8.2ft) and was not provided with drainage channels but had a very slight camber. It seems, therefore, to have been a minor **vicus** thoroughfare, taking little wheeled traffic (no ruts were visible), but allowing access to the bath-house from the civilian settlement to the north and north-west of the fort. The lowest make-up layers, immediately above the natural surface, yielded four samian vessels of Hadrianic-Antonine date and one of Antonine date indicating construction of the road c.A.D. 130-140. The paucity of Antonine pieces amongst the remaining pottery suggests that the road was not in use for long (cf. samian nos. 84- 87; coarse pottery nos. 432-7 and archive list).

The Late road.

Overlying the debris on the northern side of the early road was another road constructed of cobbles but with fewer areas of compacted surface (Fig.23, section G-F). This later road was directed not towards the bath-house but eastwards towards the river. Again, although nearly half a metre wider than the early road, it was not provided with drainage or kerbing. The pottery is predominantly Antonine but the group is 50% residual (samian nos. 88S-93; coarse pottery nos. 438-449 and archive list). Other finds included a bronze brooch, bronze tweezers and a beehive quern.

Intrusion into the early road.

Once the early road was no longer in use, it soon fell into disrepair and a number of intrusions were cut into it (features 32, 33 and 58). One cut directly across the road (32) was 1m. wide in places and had a depth of 45cms. containing rubble and dark soil. Another (33) was more hole-like, being 35cms wide and 40 cms. deep. Together, the two features yielded only four sherds of Hadrianic-Antonine date. The third intrusion (58) was more prolific. Nearly 1m. wide and 2.6m. long, it contained pottery which was predominantly Hadrianic-Antonine (including samian nos. 94; coarse pottery nos. 451-462) as well as a fragment of mirror (and other items listed in the site archive). The dates of the pottery in these intrusions confirm that the use of the early road was of short duration.

The edge of the later road was also cut in one place, although most of this intrusion had been removed by a trench dug possibly by the Rev. Mr Stevens in 1967. It yielded samian of Hadrianic-Antonine and Antonine date and second century coarse pottery (see nos 463-4).

Early road debris

On both sides of the early road, debris had accumulated up to the very edge, a further indication that this was not a major road and seems to have been poorly maintained. Over this debris of soil, stones, charcoal and pottery, the later road was laid (Fig. 23, section G-F, 6). The scarcity of Antonine relative to Hadrianic-Antonine pottery from this debris is further confirmation that the early road was probably replaced by the later c.A.D. 150 (see samian nos. 95S-99; coarse pottery nos, 465-476; coin nos.690 and 696.

The area between the path and the road.

To the south of the road lay an open area of c.35 sq.m. This was not utilised for any purpose other than the deposition of a great deal of debris and building rubble. There were no traces of any **vicus** building and the only feature was the remains of a small pit (feature 60, see below). The area must have been used as a rubbish tip, for a large amount of pottery and other finds were discovered there (samian nos. 100S-108; coarse pottery nos. 477-512A; coin no. 685; a full list of finds is in the site archive). The paucity of Antonine relative to Hadrianic-Antonine sherds would indicate that activity on this part of the site, and hence on the path and early road also, ceased c.A.D. 150. It must be noted, however, that this area was heavily disturbed in post-Roman and recent times and that many of the upper layers, containing a higher proportion of Antonine material, had to be classed as unstratified.

Pit (feature 60).

Cut into the natural clay, presumably from a much higher level, subsequently destroyed by recent activity, was the remaining part of a pit, about 1.5m. to the North of the path. Its surviving dimensions were 1.75m. x 1.3m. with a depth of 0.4m. Its fill comprised charcoal-rich soil mixed with stones and bones of cow (4 fragments), sheep (2) and pig (2). The samian from the pit is Antonine (including the stamp no.109S). The only datable coarse pottery belonged to the early third century (see nos.513-516). The glass (to be reported upon in a later volume) included window glass, a flagon and a shallow cut glass bowl.

The path.

Access from the north **vicus** to the bath-house was also provided by a path constructed of rammed pebbles lying to a depth of 30cms. directly over the natural clay. Its relationship with the road was destroyed by another 18th century stone-lined drain (Fig.23, section F-E, 3). Very few datable finds came from the path, but what there were suggested that it was contemporary with the early road (cf. samian nos. 110-111; coarse pottery nos. 517-519). One sherd joined with a vessel from the early road.

Timber trenches to the South of the path (feature 47).

Between the drainage channel (see below) and the path, and on the same alignment, was a trench for timberwork. This was 7.6m. long. Part seems to have been replaced by another trench slightly to the north. A post-hole and its replacement, both with a width of 25cms (10ins), lay at the west end of the trench. The trench presumably supported a wooden wall or fence, the function of which is unclear. If it was part of a building, no other wall parallel to it or at right angles was found. The purpose of a fence or screen in such a location and for such a short distance is also uncertain. However, the finds (coarse pottery nos. 520-524 and archival list) suggest that it ceased to function at the same time that the drainage channel went out of use.

RIBCHESTER, ACCESS ROAD 1977

Drainage channel sections

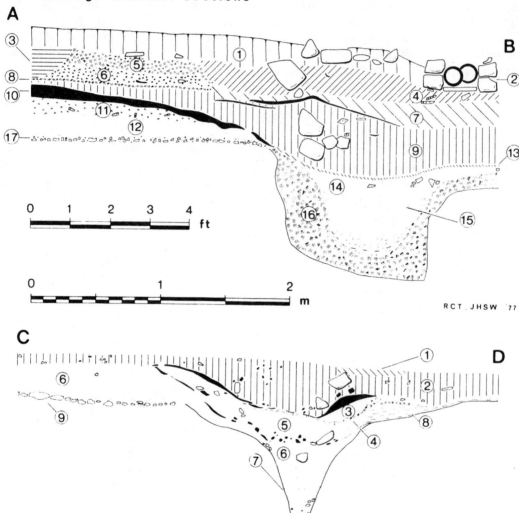

Fig.26.

The drainage channel.

Just over 2m. to the south of the timber trenches was a linear feature running in an east-west direction across the site and parallel with the north wall of the bath-house. It had a Y-shaped section and was cut into the natural clay. About 1m. wide at the top, 15cms. wide at the botton and 80cms. deep it seems to have silted up without any attempt to re-cut it (see Fig.26, section C-D). Above the primary silting (7) was a fill which consisted largely of charcoal, stones and a tip of debris from the bath-house side; this included a large amount of lead sheets and shavings. From the profile of this feature it is hard to assign it a structural function; the sides are too shallow at the top, the trench too deep. It seems too substantial to have held a palisade and no imprints or holes from timber uprights were found. The feature is likely to have been open, perhaps acting as a ditch demarcating the area of the bath-house but more probably as a watercourse.

At the west end of the excavated section, the channel seems to have cut across an earlier pit-like feature which gave the channel a rather different profile (see Fig.26, section A-B). It is possible that this is the point where it joined another watercourse coming from a slightly different direction (perhaps on a SW-NE axis) or that this wider and deeper part acted as a sump. It may be noted that a similar channel was examined in recent bath-house excavations.

Finds from the drainage channel included samian nos. 112S-120, coarse pottery nos.525-545 and coin no. 686 as well as several rings (one silver). A full list of finds appears in the site archive. From the finds it is clear that the drainage channel was accumulating rubbish in the late 1st - early 2nd century. The main filling (5 & 6) seems to have been the result of re-building work on the bath-house when the resulting debris was thrown into the channel. None of the pottery from these layers needs be later than the Hadrianic period but the presence of a few sherds of Black-burnished ware could suggest a date after c.A.D.120. The suggested date for deposition of this layer is c.A.D.130. Further debris accumulated after this (section C-D, 2; section A-B, 9) containing material of similar date but with a few Antonine pieces. The date when the channel was cut is less certain but the presence of so few purely Flavian pieces would indicate a date in the very late Flavian or even the Trajanic period.

Above the drainage channel.

Some activity at the south end of the site continued after the drainage channel was filled in. Most of the area was given over to the dumping of stones, daub and tile but in the south-west corner ephemeral traces of trenches for timber remained, suggestive perhaps of ancillary buildings relating to the maintenance of the bath-house. The South section (Fig.22, E-A, 4) also shows the presence of a daub and tile surface with a trench for timberwork flanking the east side. The pottery from this layer ranges from Flavian-Trajanic to Hadrianic-Antonine. Over this had accumulated a charcoal-rich layer which was sealed by a deposit of yellow clay. From this layer came a worn coin of Trajan (no.692) and a number of samian vessels of Flavian to Trajanic-Hadrianic date. However, all this material would seem to be residual in view of the dates from lower levels and because of the presence of a 3rd century mortarium (too incomplete to publish below).

A further feature was cut into the fill of the drainage channel; three upright flagstones enclosed a thick layer of red clay. Perhaps this was intended to form a hearth but the clay did not seem to have been burnt. The finds from the area included samian nos. 121S-123 and coarse pottery nos. 546-566.

Post-Roman activity

The Roman layers on the site had suffered considerable damage since their deposition. A few sherds of green-glazed pottery point to limited activity in the 14th-15th centuries but post-medieval damage was extensive. A soak-away and two 18th century stone-lined drains cut across the site and large intrusions were found in the stone building and the area between the path and the road. The Tithe map of 1838 (Lancashire Record Office, ref. DRB/1/164) shows that the excavated area was once part of an orchard under the ownership of James Raby and occupied by Henry Barton. Later the area seems to have been given over to allotments. Several tree-holes and areas of disturbed soil give evidence of this horticultural activity. Three field drains also cut across the site and in recent times the area became a tip for garden and household refuse, disturbing especially the most westerly part of the site near the road.

DISCUSSION AND SUMMARY.

Although a number of structures and other features were revealed in the excavation, it would be wrong to discuss them collectively in the same way that one can, for example, refer to the rebuilding of structures within a fort as belonging to a single 'phase'. The area excavated was dictated by rescue rather than research requirements. The site thus randomly selected has naturally produced **vicus** structures which would need to be seen in a much wider context to be fully understood.

The function of many of the features on the site (11b, 65-6, the trenches for timberwork and the drainage channel) cannot be interpreted with certainty and can only be dated approximately.

One assumes, for example, that the path and the early road led to the bath-house, but one cannot be sure. Where, indeed, did the later road go and why was the direction altered? This and other questions are unlikely to be answered as the area surrounding the site on the north, east and west sides consists largely of private gardens.

The following outline chronology is, however, offered:

c.A.D. 100   The cutting of the drainage channel and the construction of a timber wall parallel to it.

c.A.D. 130   The filling of the drainage channel and the demolition of the timber wall. The construction of the path and early road and the digging of clay pits to provide material for the foundations of the stone building.

by c.A.D. 140   The stone building was completed and in occupation, the clay pits and other features filled in and covered. The whole of the northern part of the site to the east of the building formed a cobble yard, perhaps delineated by a wall.

c.A.D.150   The early road fell into disuse. A barrier (feature 32) may have been constructed across it. The 'late' road headed eastwards. The timber building in the south-west corner of the site was constructed. Occupation of the stone building continued until:

c.A.D. 180/190   The end of the occupation of the stone building. Use of the later road probably continued into the third century.

Third century   A new floor was laid in the building in the south-west corner of the site. The rubbish pit (feature 60) was dug. There was limited activity connected with the slumped area of cobbling (feature 11).

An overall view of the pottery dating can be seen in the histograms (Part 3, Chapter 2, g). In general terms they both support the hypothesis that the site saw little activity in the first century, the major occupation being in the Hadrianic-Antonine period. The samian distribution shows a drop c.A.D. 160-170. The coarse pottery confirms that active interest in the area had virtually ceased after c.A.D. 180-190.

Appendix. The site archive.

The site archive to be deposited in the Lancashire Record Office contains lists of finds from major features and level details relating to the sections published here in figs.21-26.

The location of all sections is given in Fig.27 below.

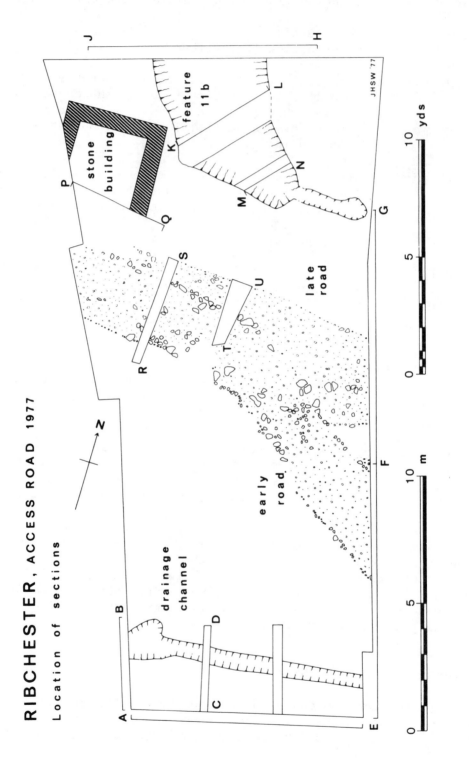

Fig.27.

Chapter 7
TRIAL EXCAVATIONS IN THE SCHOOL FIELD, 1974.
By B.J.N.Edwards & P.V.Webster.

The site of this excavation lies between the Fort bath house and the school (see Chapter 8 below). Excavation to test the potential of the site was carried out in 1974 by the authors acting for the Department of the Environment and with the cooperation of the Ribble Archaeological Society. The excavation was a response to a proposal to build a bungalow on the site and we are grateful to the then owner, Mr Hardiker for permission to excavate. The excavation strategy was designed both to sample the area and to leave space for a fuller area excavation later, if this proved necessary. In the event, the development threat receded and the land was sold. As a result of the trial excavation, the Department of the Environment decided to press for preservation rather than excavation. In the long term this is obviously the most satisfactory solution as it will preserve the site for future work, which can be undertaken without the pressure of a 'rescue' situation. In the short term, however, it does mean that a report on the 1974 excavations can only identify those areas suitable for future work and offer a very limited glimpse of the archaeology of this part of the civil settlement.

As it was virtually certain that the south end of the fort bath house lay under the northern part of the site (see plan Fig.28), trial excavation concentrated on the southern part of the site about which little was known. Here a series of hand dug trenches were cut in positions which, it was hoped, would produce a true sample of the area while leaving room for area excavation at a later date. Trenches were given letter codes in the order in which they were cut, but it will be more convenient to describe them starting with the most southerly and working north. The principle features located in all trenches are marked on the general plan (Fig.28). More detailed plans will be deposited with the site archive.

The most southerly area sampled (trench C) lay in the narrow tongue of land between the school yard (cf. Chapter 8 below) and the Duddel Brook. As in other areas, total excavation down to the natural subsoil was not attempted as the excavators envisaged an early return to the site for larger scale excavation. The lowest features excavated were two pits. Of these, one (pit C.6, 8-9) was certainly of 3rd century date (cf. pottery nos. 600-610) and was probably cut in the second half of that century. The remaining pit (C.7) yielded little which could be dated with any accuracy, but it is unlikely to be later than the other and could indeed be earlier. Sealing the pits was a levelling of mixed grey and yellow clay (C.5) which apparently formed the base for a timber building. A wall slot (C.3) ran SE/NW across the north centre of the small area opened. To the south and partially overlying it was a stone slab c.0.9 x 0.2m (3 ft x 8 ins) marking what may have been a threshold. To the east of the slot, yellow clay (C.4) formed what is assumed

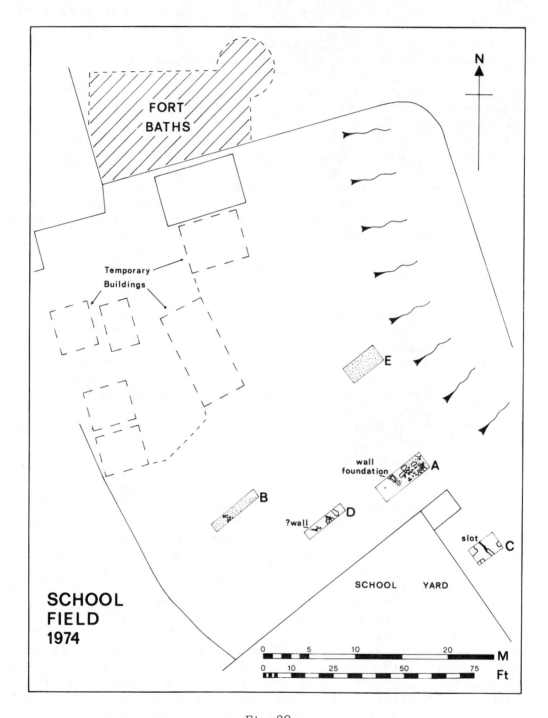

Fig.28.

to be the floor of a room. To the west, stone slabs had evidently been laid directly upon the base layer (C.5) either as the floor of a room or as the surface of a yard. Most slabs had subsequently been removed prior to the demolition of the building but three crushed examples remained in situ. Burnt clay daub (C.2) from the demolished wall lay over the slabbed surface. This destruction level included some tile which presumably indicates the method of roofing. Dating from C.5 (pottery nos. 611-3) adds little to that already provided by the pits which it seals and a late third century construction date may be suggested. Material from the demolition includes a number of pieces which may be early or mid fourth century. Demolition levels were unsealed and overlain by about 0.75m of garden soil.

The excavation of trench A (see plan Fig.28) was concentrated mainly upon a masonry building and its foundations. A small sounding of lower levels was, however, carried out and showed a layer of grey sticky clay containing plentiful charcoal (A.6), which, on the basis of excavations elsewhere, is probably to be interpreted as the destruction level of an underlying timber building. Associated pottery (samian nos. 132S-133, coarse pottery nos. 616-7) show a Flavian/Trajanic to Hadrianic range and suggests destruction in the Hadrianic period.

Above the supposed timber demolition level were the remains of what appeared to be a major masonry building. At the west end of trench A this was founded upon about 30 cms (1 ft.) of small cobble (A.5), while to the west lay a level of mixed gravel, cobble and stone blocks (A.8). The blocks measured up to 1 x 0.5m (40 x 20 ins). Above the cobble A.5 was a spread of mixed clay and humus (A.4) reminiscent of the foundation of the slab floor in trench C and possibly serving a similar purpose. This level was not present over the blocks (A.8) and was separated from them by a clay and cobble wall foundation running SE/NW (i.e. approximately the same axis as the timber building in trench C). The foundation (A.7) was 60-80 cms wide and consisted of small water worn cobbles set in orange clay. There seems little doubt that the foundation once supported a masonry wall and that this wall appears to mark the junction between an area requiring underpinning with cobble and that needing the substantial stone blocks. In part this difference may be due to the proximity of the small ravine occupied by the Duddel Brook but it may have other significance. It is possible either that the part of the building over the stone substructure was heavier (and therefore probably taller) or that the subsoil here was particularly unstable; one wonders if the eastern part of the site was not an artificial terrace formed by Roman dumping. Clearly only further excavation will resolve this particukar problem.

The excavated portion of the masonry building formed only its substructure. Above this the building had been heavily disturbed, either in demolition or subsequent gardening. However, what may be demolition debris was located in the north centre of the trench, showing a patch of clay and stone (A.2). Immediately to the west, disturbed slabs and the base of a globular amphora (A.3, a Dressel form 20 South Spanish oil amphora). marked the remains of what is probably the same deposit, possibly a heavily disturbed floor.

The sub-floor levels of the building yielded plentiful late Antonine samian together with coarse pottery of late second and third century date (nos.618-9). The latest pieces are, however, of late third century date at the earliest and this is presumably the construction date of the building. The supposed demolition levels are, of course, suspect as they have been subjected to considerable interference and were unsealed. They would, however, be compatable with demolition in the early or mid fourth century (cf. coarse pottery nos. 621-3) which seems not unreasonable given the other dating evidence from this building.

To test the extent of the masonry building, a further trench was cut from 4 to 9 metres west of the western end of trench A (Fig.28, trench D). This was excavated only onto the top of the surviving Roman features, which appeared at depths varying between 0.45 and 0.8m. An area of burnt clay or daub and of tumbled stone blocks was revealed, together with what may be the top of a further stone wall, perhaps with some of its stone blocks in position c. 10m (32.8 ft.) west of the foundation A.7. As it seemed highly probable that the masonry building extended into area D, no further work was attempted here, as only large scale area excavation seemed likely to produce meaningful details of such a disturbed, but clearly important building.

Also possibly relevant to the masonry building is a small area (trench E) opened to the north (see Fig.28). This revealed heavy cobble within 20cms of the surface. Here, at least, later gardening does not seem to have removed or even disturbed the latest Roman levels. It is tempting to associate the cobble with a yard attached to the masonry building or with a road serving it and linking it to the bath house. Whichever ultimately proves to be the case, the area is clearly potentially useful in view of the apparently undisturbed nature of the deposits. As in the case of trench D, having established the potential of the area trench E was not excavated further in anticipation of later larger scale work.

The final trench to be considered tested the western extremities of the site (B see Fig.28). The lowest levels excavated (B.8) consisted of grey sand, clay and gravel, cut by a slot at the west end of the trench. At this stage, therefore, the area probably contained timber buildings. As B.8 was not in fact penetrated by the trial excavations no firm date can be assigned to it, but in view of the likely date of subsequent levels a late first or early second century date seems probable. Over the building level were two distinct surfaces of cobble (B.7 over B.7a). These seem likely to belong to a road linking the fort and the baths. Dating evidence was slight but the absence of Black-burnished ware may imply an early second century date. Subsequently the road appears to have been deliberately cambered by adding a level of grey clay (B.6), about 10 cms thick towards the centre of the road and thinning to neglible dimensions towards its edges. Above the clay, along what may be the centre line of the road, lay some larger blocks of stone up to 25 cms in length; either side of these lay light cobble (B.5). The edge of this supposed road was located to the east and ran approximately SE/NW. The clay road yielded a mortarium fragment and Antonine samian. Above the road lay burnt daub and other debris (B.2, B.4)indicating the position of a demolished timber building. No building slots were identified and it is possible, therefore, that the building from which the debris derived and which presumably edged the roadway only impinged upon it at demolition stage. The pottery fron the demolition deposit (nos. 624-9) show that it is late second century at the earliest and more probably of early third century date.

To summarise, the trial excavations in the School Field suggest that this is an area of considerable archaeological potential. Excavations showed that during the third and early fourth centuries the area contained a number of buildings, all aligned similarly along a NE/SW axis and apparently including at least one large masonry building. With the exception of the bath house (which, of course, impinges on the northern end of the site), no other large masonry building in the civil settlement is known although at least one other can be assumed (the temple cf. RIB 587). The masonry building is likely, therefore, to have been a structure of particular importance in the civil settlement. If we may presume that Ribchester once possessed a **mansio**, could this be it? Certainly the position close to the baths and near the fort would be suitable and the relatively high proportion of fine wares among the finds would be appropriate. Clearly only future excavation can test this piece of speculation but, even if it were proved wrong, the rarity of third and fourth century occupation elsewhere in the civil settlement makes this an important area.

RIBCHESTER

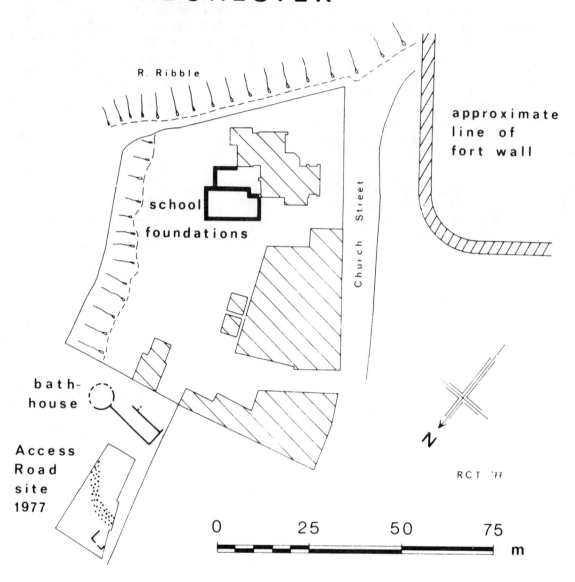

Fig.29.

Chapter 8
THE PRIMARY SCHOOL FOUNDATION TRENCHES, 1977
By R.C.Turner & J.H.S.Witherington.

During the excavation of the Access Road site construction work began on the foundations for an extension to the Ribchester Church of England Primary School (see Fig.29). Apart from the small scale work in 1974 a few metres to the east (see Chapter 7 above), the area in which the trenches were located had been largely unexplored. Its proximity to the fort made it important to carry out a watching brief on the machine work.

The authors acknowledge the generous assistance of the builder, Mr J.Green of Accrington and his staff, who facilitated in every way the difficult task of rescuing material and recording stratigraphic information. They would also like to thank the Headmaster, Mr Fisher, for his helpful cooperation. The retrieval was carried out by members of the team then at work on the Access Road site (Chapter 6 above) and the finds were processed by Miss Helen Lockwood. We are in the debt of Mr J.Blundell and his staff of the Lancashire County Museums Service for conserving the large amount of organic material so promptly after its recovery. Post-excavation work was assisted by a grant from the Department of the Environment and facilities and services were provided by the Department of Classics and Archaeology, University of Lancaster. The debt owed to writers of specialist reports will be evident both from this chapter and in later parts in this series where their reports will appear.

The two southernmost trenches (Fig.29) were dug to a depth of c.1.5m and yielded only a handful of sherds. The section (Fig.30, C-D) showed that the upper layers consisted of recent material derived from the digging of the first school extension in 1967 and from a number of more recent drains (C-D,1). The Roman layers were sealed by a 26 cm. deposit of gravel and cobble (C-D,2) and consisted of a ditch-like feature cut through grey occupation material (C-D,7). The sides of the ditch carried a tip of mixed red clay, daub and charcoal (C-D,4). Over this a fine grey silt had accumulated (C-D,3). The exact nature of the ditch could not be determined as the trench itself was not excavated beyond the depth required by the builder. Its alignment was approximately NW-SE and it did not reappear in any of the other trenches.

The northernmost trench (Fig.30, E-F) was also machine-dug to a depth of c.1.5m., but it was clear from the amount of samian and coarse pottery being retrieved and the nature of the layers from which they came, that further work should be carried out manually. This was made possible by the helpful cooperation of the builder.

The original ground surface sloped down north-eastwards towards the river and from the evidence of the eastern end of the trench (see fig.30, E-F), the slope seems to have been levelled off

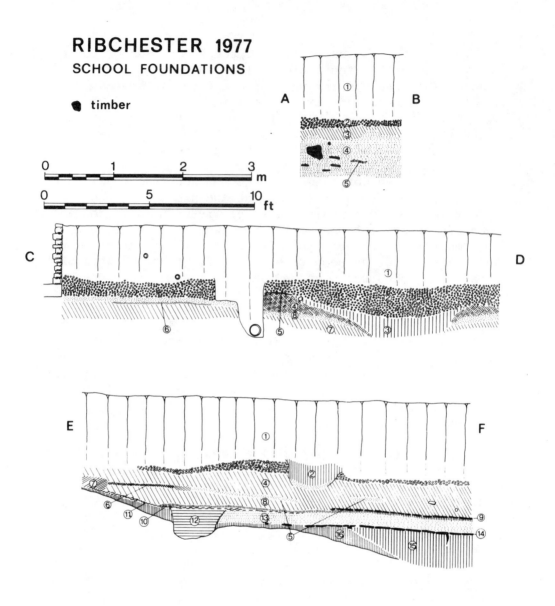

RIBCHESTER 1977
SCHOOL FOUNDATIONS

● timber

Fig.30.

with a thick layer of soft, clean grey clay (E-F,15). Over this had been laid a floor of timber planking, in places with upright stakes or horizontal wooden supports (E-F,14). Over this floor a 20 cm. layer of grey occupation material had been built up with a more concentrated charcoal fill at the western end (E-F,13). Over this had been laid a thin sealing layer of grey clay (E.F-10) which provided a more secure base for a second floor, again of timber (E-F,9). Another layer of mixed occupation material (E-F,4 & 8) accumulated before the whole area was covered by a deposit of gravel and small cobbles (E-F,3). In this layer one small pit-like intrusion was identified, filled with grey silt and pebbles (E-F,2).

The western half of this section differs from the half already described in that it lacks the two floors, although two separate occupation horizons were still evident. After the construction of the first floor and the build-up of material, but before the laying down of the second floor, a small pit had been dug into the natural ground surface and was filled with a very dry peaty soil (E-F,12). A thin layer of what appeared to be wood shavings had accumulated over and around the pit (E-F,11). The upper levels of the trench again consisted of recent building disturbance and rubble beneath the tarmac of the school playground (E-F,1).

One further section was recorded (Fig.30, A-B) where a large wooden beam running across the line of the trench had been snapped off by the machine. Here the beam and other pieces of wood lay in a peaty soil with lenses of grey silt (A-B,4 & 5). Again the levels were sealed by a 20cm. deposit of gravel (A-B,2)

DISCUSSION.

a) Chronology.

Because of the conditions under which the finds were recovered, the exact stratigraphical context is known for only a few items. As a result, the material has to be treated as unstratified and only general conclusions can be drawn.

To display the collection of pottery as a whole, a histogram has been drawn of the datable pieces (Fig. 31) showing the chronological distribution of the samian and coarseware separately. To construct this diagram each datable sherd was given a score of one. In the case of the samian this score was divided equally over the stated date range into five year periods. Because coarse ware can be less accurately dated, the score is divided into ten year periods.

There are obvious limitations to this method. Firstly, it is known that samian was available in larger quantities in some periods relative to others. This can be seen most readily if the Flavian and Antonine periods are contrasted to the Trajanic, a

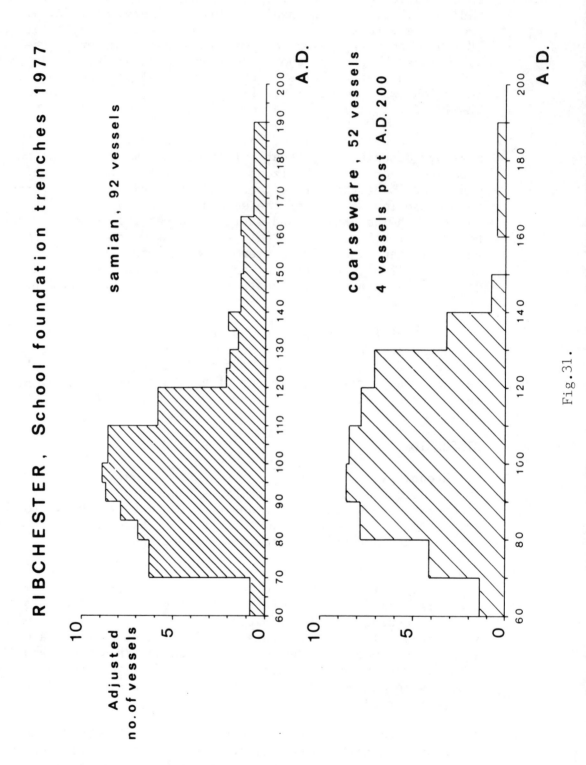

RIBCHESTER, School foundation trenches 1977

samian, 92 vessels

coarseware, 52 vessels
4 vessels post A.D. 200

Fig.31.

constant and no break in occupation can be detected. It is, therefore, impossible to date the second phase of wooden building with any accuracy.

Both histograms show that pottery later than A.D.130 is present on the site. In proportion to the earlier periods the amount is quite small and it is not unreasonable to assume that it came from nearby occupied areas after the deposition of gravel.

b) The Building.
Structural evidence for the nature of the building is meagre. No rubble foundations, post-holes or beam trenches came into the excavated section and only details of the oak and pine flooring survived. That no plan could be obtained was all the more unfortunate as wooden structures so well preserved are rare. The building lies about 45m to the north of the north-east fort gate. So far as it known, the outline of the timber fort on this side is the same as the subsequent stone one, although the 1980 excavations to the north of the stone fort showed that this need not necessarily be so and there is, of course, evidence for a substantial rearrangement of the internal fort buildings (cf. Edwards & Webster 1985, p.6 & pp.38-47). The building is, therefore, presumably in the **vicus** and its civilian nature is not negated by the bracelet and spindle found in it (to be reported upon in Part 4 of this series). Among the other finds there was nothing diagnostic which could point to a particular purpose for the building. Two factors, however, indicate an unexpected degree of affluence amongst the occupants. The quality of samian and even some of the coarseware far exceeds that of comparable material from the Access Road site and the proportion of samian to coarseware is unusually high. While the first could point to a military rather than a civilian presence (part of an annexe, for example), the second seems atypical of a military context. The indications are, therefore, inconclusive even without taking into account the distortions of a machine excavated sample.

c) Conclusions.
The similarity between this **vicus** building and structures on the north-west side of the fort (above, Chapter 2) is immediately apparent. Both were built in the early 80's or soon after; both had short periods of occupation, ending in demolition and a superimposed gravel spread. That extra-mural buildings should spring up so quickly after the foundation of the fort is not unusual. Watercrook provides a similar example (Potter 1979, p.139 ff.). The clearing of areas close to the fort may well be linked to a change in the nature or number of the garrison. In the case of the area under discussion clearance took place c.A.D.120-5. Unusual features in the overall numismatic picture also hint at changes in this period (see Edwards & Webster 1985, pp.88-9; also ibid.p.38). A suitable context for such activity is the setting up of the Hadrianic frontier which will have entailed a large scale redeployment of troops. This inevitably affected the lives of those

period during which the sources of supply were moving from South to Central Gaul and when supplies appear to have been reduced. Such variations in supply will always affect the shape of a histogram of this type. Secondly, dates for samian are often not given in years but in more general imperial periods, e.g. 'Flavian-Trajanic'. When such dates are converted into calendar years, it tends to be reflected in the histogram by sudden variations at the end of the major imperial dynasties (i.e. at the close of the Flavian, Trajanic, Hadrianic and Antonine periods). Thirdly, the date ranges for the coarseware come almost exclusively from J.P.Gillam's typology (Gillam 1970, 1976), hence any distribution will be affected by its strengths and weaknesses. The more easily identifiable types and fabrics will tend to be over-represented. With coarsewares of this region there are always false peaks for the periods A.D.70-160 and A.D.370-400. These result from the way in which Gillam's typology is constructed where groups of pottery which could be dated by external means were taken and compared. The very varied and comparatively well known history of the frontier region in the period A.D.70-160 and the hiatus of the Pictish War in A.D.367-9 has led to a much higher number of these crucial groups being used rather than those of the period A.D.160-370 for which far less evidence is available

Finally it is worth noting that coarseware tends to have a shorter life than fineware and, because of the way in which Gillam's typology is built, the given date range of a vessel will quite accurately reflect its 'discard' date. In the case of samian, however, the given range more accurately reflects the period of manufacture and, because of the longer life of samian vessels, the 'discard' date will tend to be towards the end of the given range or even outside it. Thus, in attempting to fix the approximate chronological limits of occupation of the building, the coarse ware should be a better guide for the starting date, the samian for the closing date. For this reason there are two separate histograms.

For the beginning of occupation on the site, the two histograms would indicate a date in the early 80's. The presence of only four samian vessels of form Drag.29 would suggest that the date is unlikely to be earlier and this does not contradict the evidence of other samian pieces which are known to be from the first phase of occupation or below it.

For the end of the occupation of the buildings, the two types of pottery would suggest slightly dissimilar dates. Quantities of samian fall off sharply at the end of Trajan's reign, c.A.D.120, while the coarseware drops markedly from A.D.130 onwards. However, the coarse pottery contains very few sherds of Black-burnished ware, so prevalent in the North after c.A.D.120 and it would, therefore, seem likely that the end of the building's life belongs to the period A.D.120-125. The coin of A.D.116 (no.702) would not contradict this. Thus we have a maximum occupation period of about 45 years between A.D.80 and A.D.125 during which the structure seems to have been rebuilt once. Between these two dates, the rate of loss of pottery seems to be fairly

RIBCHESTER

SCHOOL FOUNDATION TRENCHES 1977

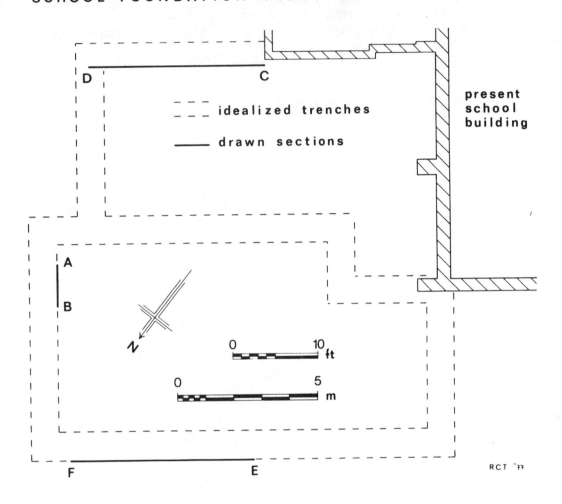

Fig.32.

in the civil settlement ar Ribchester as well as in other extra-mural settlements in northern Britain. It must, however, be noted that, although the present excavations, those in the Playing field (Chapter 2) and those immediately north of the stone fort (Edwards & Webster 1985, p.47) all show evidence for the levelling and clearance of areas close to the fort, there is as yet no consistency in the dating of that clearance, although it would be possible to argue for a gradual increase in the area cleared between the later first and the later second century on the basis of the three excavations. Clearly we must await more work on this particular problem.

Chapter 9
POSTSCRIPT: THE NATURE OF THE RIBCHESTER CIVIL SETTLEMENT
By A.C.H.Olivier

Much of the discussion regarding the nature of the minor settlements in this country encompassed by the broad definition of the term 'vicus' (Wacher 1974, pp.14-21; Johnson 1975, pp.75-79; Salway 1980, pp.8-10 & 1981, pp.590-591; Sommer 1984, p.53) has centred on the origin and development of the so-called 'small town' in the Midlands, the south, and the east (Todd 1970, pp.114-130; Rodwell and Rowley 1974; Millet 1984, pp.65-75). It has often been assumed (Millet 1984, p.65) that the differing circumstances of military control will have exercised a significant effect on the development of such settlements in the north where 'vici around northern forts represent an early stage of development, crystallised throughout the Roman period in the form in which they began' (Johnson 1975, p.75). Salway, however, has questioned the whole concept of the frontier region of Roman Britain being under a formally constituted military administration (1980, p.10), and by implication, therefore, suggests that an explanation of the differences in the development of northern and southern vici should perhaps be sought elsewhere.

Detailed information regarding the exact nature of extra-mural activity associated with Roman forts is best derived from large scale area excavation. However, in spite of a number of projects undertaken in the north in recent years, and with a few notable exceptions, our understanding of such sites has advanced little since 1973, when Birley lamented our general lack of knowledge (1973, p.31). In particular, until fairly recently it was assumed that civil settlements in the frontier region dependent upon a fort were undefended, and generally did not exceed c.10 acres in size. Anomalies such as Corbridge had to be regarded as exceptional (Salway 1965, p.41). At Kirkby Thore, originally thought to be defended, the results of excavations in 1964 (Charlesworth 1964, pp.426-427) and 1983 (Gibbons forthcoming) suggest that evidence for a defended settlement or small town cannot be substantiated, and consequently that estimates of the extent of extra-mural activity at that location are erroneous.

However, defences associated with extra-mural activity have now been identified at a number of sites, including both Chesterholm/Vindolanda (Birley 1977) and Melandra (Webster 1971) and it has been suggested that these settlements may have reached a stage in their development when they merited a legally higher status as well as the presence of defences (Jones & Walker 1983, p.190). In the case of Chesterholm, however, the supposed defended settlement may actually have been part of a military annexe attached to the fort (Salway 1980, p.15), and it is clear that the presence of defences may be open to a number of differing, and perhaps conflicting interpretations. Nevertheless, surveys of both Romano-British urban defences (Crickmore 1984) and 'military vici' in Roman Britain (Sommer 1984), demonstrate that, as a result of the increased number of excavations undertaken in recent years, the association of defences with extra-mural occupation, although still unusual in northern England, is by no means as exceptional today as was supposed in the past.

Our knowledge of the role of such defences and their relationship (if any) with interior features is still slight, and it has already been seen that they may have had a purely military function, defining an annexe attached to a fort rather than supposedly conventional civil occupation (at many sites such differences have yet to be defined adequately by excavation). It is also possible that unassociated defences may, of course, relate to hitherto unrecorded forts of different size or date. The techniques employed in the construction of these defences were also diverse, perhaps emphasising a wide range of function rather than a single easily identified class of site, or that they were perhaps the work of builders without military training. In spite of these problems, however, the presence of defences associated (in some way) with extra-mural occupation at Chesterholm (op.cit.), Melandra (op.cit.), Slack (Hunter, Manby & Spaul 1971, pp.83-87), Manchester (**Britannia** 10 (1979) p.291), Malton (Ramm 1978, pp.63-68), Ilkley (Salway 1965, p.41), Doncaster (Buckland and Magilton 1986), and possibly Greta Bridge (**Britannia** 6 (1975) p.235) and Llanio (**Britannia** 1 (1970) p.269) suggests that some such settlements, at least, are likely to have been defended or defined by earthwork enclosures.

The presence of defences discovered outside the fort at Ribchester may, therefore, relate to either a defended military annexe, or a civil settlement, or indeed serve some other purpose such as outworks (Wilson 1984, pp.51-61). Certainly, in the north, annexes to forts are less rare than defences bounding extra-mural occupation, and at Ribchester the defences could have defined a large military compound (including a bath-house), rather than a civil settlement. These defences, however, are slight, and generally unmilitary in character, and there are no clear indications concerning their origin or function. Defences outside extra-mural civil settlements may not, however, be particularly unusual, and the limited number of examples may simply be a product of the small number of excavations located (fortuitously or otherwise) at the edge of such settlements.

Whether defences around extra-mural civil settlements were originally a fairly common feature (requiring little or no specific explanation), or whether they were exceptional (perhaps indicating local requirements or particular status), it is likely that their presence will have been inextricably intertwined with the function and status of the settlements they bounded (Wacher 1974, p.20). Unfortunately, many of the questions related to this fundamental issue remain unresolved, particularly for such settlements in the north of England. In addition, whilst civil settlements in the north have many attributes in common, it is by no means clear that they should always be classified together and treated as an homogenous group any more than other minor settlements (Todd 1970, p.115). Indeed, data derived from excavation suggests that the variations between individual sites are quite as striking as the similarities.

The term **vicus** has a wide range of meanings, not necessarily consistent throughout the Empire either chronologically or geographically (Johnson 1975, p.75), and includes a subdivision or ward of a town (Wacher 1974, p.13; Salway 1980, p.8 & 1981, pp.590-591), as well as an independent division within a large household (Johnson op.cit.). Generally, however, a **vicus** may be taken to define a small settlement of village size, without any form of self government, and subordinate to the administration of another larger town in the neighbourhood (ibid.). The **vicus**, therefore, may be regarded as part of a settlement hierarchy ranging from an individual farmstead to a town (Jones 1984, p.76). Johnson indicates that these small communities were usually unwalled (op.cit.), Wacher, however, suggests that many 'small towns' probably also held the status of **vicus**, as well as nucleated but unfortified settlements, and that the term was, therefore, applied to both defended and undefended (village sized) settlements (1974, p.14). In the north, the range of known settlement types is much more limited (Jones op.cit.), possibly as a result of the influence of the military authorities. Nevertheless, a number of inscriptions (Salway 1965, pp.10-11) indicate that the status of most civil settlements outside forts is likely to have been that of a **vicus**. Such sites represent the most common form of Romanised settlement in the region, and are often regarded as a valid urban, or at least semi-urban, form (Salway 1980, p.8). These settlements are, therefore, often described as **vici**, although the distinction between civilian and military activity is frequently not apparent. Johnson has also warned that there is no evidence for contemporary use of the word **vicus** in Britain after the second century, and consequently that considerable care must be taken in applying the term to any site occupied after that date (1979, pp.79-80).

In Italy, **vici** developed a commercial role as small markets dependent upon local cult centres generally positioned at cross-roads, and the term was later applied, during the incorporation of newly occupied territories, to either newly formed or pre-existing small settlements (Johnson 1980, p.77). In northern England (where attention has already been drawn to the more limited range of settlement forms), the location of civil nucleated settlement is invariably dependent upon, and linked throughout its existence, to the site of a fort. There is, however, little direct evidence (either documentary or archaeological) regarding the role of such settlements, which may not necessarily have been the same as that of settlements of probably equal status either in lowland England or on the continent. Many of the specific problems relating to this issue have recently been summarised and discussed by Casey (1982) and others (Birley 1973; Salway 1980; Breeze 1982; Jones 1984; Sommer 1984), and it is clear that the available data provide insufficient grounds for anything other than the broadest general conclusions.

In spite of such difficulties, it is generally assumed that extra-mural settlements were economically dependent on the forts with which they were so closely associated geographically; the details of this relationship, and the direction of dependence, however, have yet to be determined fully. Whilst both the size of the Roman military garrison in the north and its constant requirement for supplies was considerable (Breeze 1982), its economic impact on the region is by no means certain. Although the cumulative economic effect of the military presence may have been enormous (ibid. p.159), recent work suggests that for the country as a whole, not only the economic burden, but also the social effect of the Roman army may have been less pronounced than is often supposed (Millet 1984, pp.68-9). The extent to which existing settlement patterns, agricultural practices and traditions were affected by the presence of the Roman army have all recently been addressed elsewhere (Manning 1975; Higham 1982; Jones and Walker 1983; Jones 1984). In spite of a considerable body of circumstantial evidence to the contrary, there is, however, little direct evidence for a close economic relationship between forts, their **vici**, and agricultural sites (Casey 1982, p.124 & 129).

Many questions concerning both the status and occupation of the **vicani** also remain unanswered, and a number of problems relating to the construction, ownership and tenancy of **vici** have yet to be resolved (Casey 1982; Jones 1984, p.84), although the involvement of the Roman army in these spheres of activity may have been under-estimated (Casey op.cit.). It is unclear to what extent the **vicani** may have been dependent on the pay of the associated garrison, and there is no general consensus regarding the possible degree of economic stimulation or otherwise provided by such pay. The population of a **vicus** may, therefore, have included any combination of officials, priests, traders, merchants, farmers, domestics and servants, prostitutes, veterans and various dependants, all linked to a lesser or greater extent to the serving soldiers resident in the fort.

The proportion of inhabitants occupying a particular role will of course have been dependent on the various functions of the **vicus**. These functions may, therefore, have included that of a market place, whose primary purpose was supplying a garrison with its food, derived from the hinterland of the fort, and a secondary role of providing goods and services to individual soldiers. In this respect, although economically dependent on a fort, such a settlement would have filled a broadly parallel role to sites of similar status in the South, as well as on the continent. It should be emphasised, however, that the mechanisms of supply and exchange relating to the Roman army were both complex and multifarious, and that no simple pattern emerges from the documentary evidence (Breeze 1982). The function of a **vicus** may, on the other hand, have been much more directly related to the role of the garrison. These ancilliary settlements could have been planned, constructed, owned and administered by the army, and perhaps largely populated by dependants and/or veterans (Casey 1982). In this instance, the **vicus** would have had little independent existence, and may in fact have been almost entirely dependent on the adjacent fort for supplies and commodities. At Chesterholm/Vindolanda, it has been suggested that Vicus I, bounded by defences (Birley 1977), was not comparable to the more usual form of extra-mural settlement, but may have been an official administrative station (Salway 1980). The existence of other similar compounds in the region should not be ruled out. Nevertheless, the presence within extra-mural settlements of official buildings including temples, bath-houses and possibly the so-called 'mansiones' (Salway 1980, p.10; Jones 1984, pp.78-79) alongside domestic and, in many cases, apparently commercial structures, at least indicates some plurality of function.

In the absence of any clear understanding of the economic and commercial role of **vici**, no causal relationship between the function and status of these sites can be established with confidence. The presence of defences may well be indicative of increased status derived from commercial success (Jones 1984, p.79), even fullfilling the specific commercial function of controlling traffic and trade, and facilitating the collection of taxes and duties at gateways. Conversely, they may be related to other entirely non-commercial, perhaps military, factors. Consequently, the existence of an additional line of defences c.200m north of the fort at Ribchester necessitates at least some re-appraisal of the character and nature of extra-mural occupation there.

Unfortunately, it is neither possible to define what was enclosed by the new defences recorded in 1980, nor to estimate the size of the area enclosed. With the exception of the insubstantial industrial activity described above, there is no direct link with the extra-mural settlement. Indeed, these defences may actually relate to some some other hitherto undefined or unrecorded activity at Ribchester (perhaps an annexe to the fort?). Although the fort is known to have continued in occupation until the fourth century (Frere 1967, pp.235-6; Edwards 1972; Edwards and Webster 1985, p.16), and the presence of pottery and coins suggests broadly contemporary activity in places outside the fort, with the exception of the bathhouse and its vicinity, no structures of third or fourth century date have yet been recorded. No standing structures recorded during the 1980 excavations were contemporary with the defences, and whilst their dating may be unreliable (above), it is not possible to demonstrate the existence of any substantial contemporary occupation or activity. Consequently, the status and function of these defences, and their relationship with other activity at Ribchester, remains open to question.

The reason for the establishment of defences enclosing (or defining) the area of Ribchester now in the vicinity of Parsonage Avenue also remains unknown. The widespread construction of earthwork urban defences in this country during the second half of the second century A.D. is well attested, and has been the subject of considerable discussion (most recently Crickmore 1984, pp.12-16; Frere 1984, p.63). It is generally agreed that the majority of such earthworks were the result of either a concerted programme, or a chain reaction and that they seldom reflected a specific response to local events (loc.cit.; Wacher 1975, p.51). The inclusion in this apparent programme of a large number of settlements with the presumed status of **vicus** as well as the more important self-governing centres has been emphasised by Frere who concludes that

civic pride or rivalry is unlikely to have been the motive for the
construction of defences around individual settlements (op.cit.).
The presence at Ribchester of earthwork defences of comparable date
(phase 1 - late Antonine) may, therefore, be part of such an
officially sanctioned (if not inspired) programme, rather than
related to the status or function of the settlement outside the
fort.

The dating evidence associated with both phases of defences
at Ribchester is rather limited, and it is not possible to define
the specific late second century context in which the phase 1
defences may have been constructed (op.cit., pp.71-72). It is also
unclear how the phase 2 (earthwork) defences may relate to the
general and fairly continuous trend of construction of masonry walls
around many towns and smaller settlements from c.A.D.220 until
c.A.D.360 (Wacher 1975, p.51). This trend was presumably also the
result of deliberate policy, although many details regarding its
context, chronology and development have yet to be fully resolved
(Crickmore 1984, pp.16-18). It is interesting to note, however, that
the fort was replanned during this period (the early third century).

In the north, there is little specific information available
related to the so-called Brigantian revolt of the mid second century
A.D., described by Pausanias (Salway 1965, pp.184-188, 1981, pp.199
ff; Hartley 1980, pp.5-6; Frere 1974; Hind 1977). The extent of the
Brigantian **civitas**, the status of the area north of Hadrian's Wall
and its relationship with the rest of Brigantia, the susceptibility
of all (or part) of the tribe to Roman occupation, and the confident
identification of the ('Genounian') areas involved in the attack or
revolt, are all issues that require further clarification. The
continued presence of garrisons west of the Pennines may possibly
indicate unrest in that part of the region at least (Hartley 1980,
p.5), although there is little evidence that the pattern of forts in
northern England suggests a response to the intransigence of the
local inhabitants at any time after their conquest (Breeze and
Dobson 1985, p.19). Whilst some of the consequences of this revolt
have been firmly established - a large part of the Brigantian
territory was confiscated by the Emperor (Salway 1980, p.13), the
exact date is still open to dispute (loc.cit.), and it is,
therefore, not apparent how these events may have interrelated (if
at all) with the re-occupation and subsequent abandonment of
southern Scotland (Salway 1965 & 1981; Breeze & Dobson 1978; Hartley
1980). Reservations have also been expressed regarding the actual
authenticity of the 'Brigantian Revolt' (Breeze and Dobson 1978,
pp.105-108, and 1985, p.11 n.52).

The degree to which any of these incidents or other later
military problems on the frontier (Hartley 1980, p.6) may have
affected Ribchester, situated well to the south, cannot be assessed.
Nonetheless, whilst the presence of the defences at Ribchester may
be entirely unrelated to the issues described above, it is evident
that such defences may not necessarily be out of place in the
general context of the military situation in the north during the
latter part of the second century A.D. The refurbished defences

(third century A.D.) may, on the other hand, reflect the greater prosperity of the military dependent **vici** under the Severi (Salway 1965, pp.187–188), although at Ribchester there is an almost complete lack of context for these defences. Indeed, neither phase of the defences would have presented a serious military obstacle to an aggressor, particularly with regard to the size and apparently open nature of the area enclosed, and they may not have been defences in the full sense of the word, but rather a form of settlement boundary.

The long occupation of the fort at Ribchester presumably reflects the importance of its position at the western end of a main cross-route linking the two important north-south roads on either side of the Pennines that provided access to the northern frontier (Breeze and Dobson 1985, p.18). The location of the fort at such a major road junction may have been sufficient reason for the extensive extra-mural activity there; the presence of defences possibly associated with that activity may, therefore, be the product (direct or otherwise) of the importance of that location, rather than an indication of any particular or exceptional status or function that may be ascribed to the fort. It has already been seen that it is difficult to make even a general assessment of the nature or role of the civil settlement at Ribchester against the background of similar settlements in the north. Nevertheless, there has already been sufficient discussion of the possible distinct and unusual status of the fort there to allow a consideration of the defences recorded in 1980, in relation to these issues (Richmond 1945; Holder 1982; Breeze & Dobson 1985).

Two inscriptions (RIB 587 and RIB 583), both apparently from extra-mural shrines or monuments, suggest that the fort at Ribchester may have had an extraordinary status and function (Richmond 1945). The first (RIB 587) dated between A.D.225 and A.D.235 identifies a legionary centurion as commanding both an auxiliary unit (a **numerus**), and (unusually) a wider sphere of command (signified by **regi[onis]**). The military or geopolitical implications of such a command and the possible duties involved have been discussed in detail by Richmond (op.cit.) and others, but are by no means clear. the second inscription (RIB 583) dated A.D.241, identifies the garrison of the fort at that time as a **numerus** of Sarmatian cavalry. The levy by Marcus Aurelius in A.D.175 of 8000 Sarmatian heavy cavalry and the subsequent dispatch of 5500 of them to Britain is well known (Salway 1981, pp.207–208), and the unit identified at Ribchester has often been regarded as part of this force (Richmond 1945; Salway 1965, p.29; Holder 1982, p.17; Simpson 1985, p.16). However, with the exception of this unit, there is little other direct evidence of Sarmatians in this country, and the remainder of the force may not have remained in Britain long (Frere 1967, p.162; Holder op.cit.). Indeed, it is not proven that the **numerus** stationed at Ribchester was originally part of this levy, or if it came to Britain at a different time (Breeze and Dobson, 1985, p.13).

The somewhat unusual circumstances surrounding this force,

and in particular the failure of Marcus Aurelius' plan to create a new province of Sarmatia, led Richmond to conclude that on their discharge they may have been accorded special status and then settled **en bloc** in a single district of their adopted province. Ribchester and its adjacent region, through its association with Sarmatians, was seen as a particularly suitable candidate for such settlement. The unusual presence of a legionary **regionarius** presumably responsible for more than simply the fort and its **territorium**, together with the later identification in the Ravenna Cosmography of Ribchester as a rare example of a veteran settlement, and the existence of both a monument and a temple indicating a possible religious centre, were regarded by Richmond as further corroboration of this hypothesis. In the absence of any firm evidence within the extra-mural settlement of extensive veteran settlement of an urban or at least semi-urban nature, Richmond suggested that the veterans would mainly have been concerned with land development, probably in the Fylde, where they may have been involved both in improving and draining the marshlands, and rearing horses. The **regio** (RIB 587) associated with the fort was, therefore, seen by Richmond as comprising three separate political entities, all under the authority of the **regionarius** - the Sarmatian veterans, working the Fylde, the **vicani**, living within the **territorium** of the fort, and the indigenous inhabitants of the general area.

Without a doubt, there is clear epigrapahic evidence to the effect that both the status and function of the fort at Ribchester were rather exceptional, and this is confirmed by the presumed existence of an important temple and substantial monument. In general, however, this political status is not reflected (and perhaps would not necessarily be apparent) archaeologically. The results of excavations either inside or outside the fort only differ from comparable sites in the north in matters of detail. Although the fort is certainly linked with a **numerus** of Sarmatian cavalry in the middle third century A.D., any association either with the levy of A.D.175, or with the possible, but undocumented settlement in this country of veterans derived from that levy remains entirely circumstantial. It is interesting to note, however, that the closing of the **retentura** of the fort also occurred at this time (c.A.D. 200), and consequently this remodelling of the fort could also be linked to the presence of Sarmatians during this period. Fieldwork and aerial reconnaissance of the Fylde have produced little evidence for any extensive Roman activity in that area. Whether Ribchester, rather than the Roman fort at Kirkham, would be a suitable administrative centre for officially sanctioned settlement in the Fylde may also be questioned (Sommer 1984, p.29).

There is also insufficient evidence presently available to suggest that large numbers of Sarmatian veterans were settled immediately outside the fort at Ribchester. It is certainly possible that the erection of boundary defences during the late Antonine period may define an annexe to the fort perhaps constructed on the arrival of the Sarmatian garrison. At least a part of the area thus enclosed formed a large open gravelled space, that replaced earlier structures to the north of the fort (Edwards 1972, p.14). The refurbishment of those defences during the third century A.D. could be associated with the continued use either of such an annexe, or of the earlier possible veteran settlement, that was at least semi-urban in nature, and reflecting a status not recorded elsewhere in the north. It should be emphasised, however, that there is no evidence for an extensive settlement of that date outside the fort, in those areas of Ribchester sampled by excavation. Also, whilst the unusual status of the garrison commander at Ribchester is undoubted, there is no specific link between that officer and the presence of Sarmatian cavalry, and that the association of Ribchester with any form of officially organised Sarmatian veteran settlement is unproven.

Recently, much of the accepted interpretation of the later phases of the military history of Roman Britain has been called into question (Welsby 1982, p.2). Unfortunately, the general picture remains confused, and there is considerable uncertainty regarding the military position in the north of England, particularly between the years A.D.280 and 370 (ibid.; Breeze and Dobson 1985, p.16). At Ribchester, in spite of a growing body of material indicative of activity within the fort during the later third and early fourth centuries (Edwards and Webster 1985, pp.16, 38-40, 46, 89-90), few details are known. Certainly the fort defences were remodelled at some time during this period (Edwards 1972, p.7) and although the exact context or date of such work is unclear, most forts in the north of Britain show evidence of rebuilding at this time (Welsby 1982, pp.68-90). Casey has discussed the problems associated with the abandonment or possible resiting of vici (1982, p.128). Whether the apparently deliberate slighting and sealing of the extra-mural defences at Ribchester was associated with any such official clearance at this location is unknown, and it has been seen that the available dating evidence for those defences is generally inconsistent with occupation of the known settlement outside the fort. Nevertheless, whatever their function, the considerable effort expended in razing those defences some time during the first half of the fourth century A.D. suggests some form of official action, perhaps associated with the major and contemporary remodelling of the fort defences in order to provide an unobstructed view and clear field of fire north of the fort. activity which also included the closing of the West gate of the fort (Edwards & Webster 1985, pp.26-27).

It has already been seen that the presence of defences around extra-mural settlement may not necessarily have been exceptional, and certainly could have been the product of a variety of factors or circumstances current in the north during the late second and third centuries A.D. Nevertheless, whilst the existence of such defences is yet relatively rare in the archaeological record, their occurrence at Ribchester should be taken as a further indication and archaeological confirmation of the importance and unusual status of that fort, consistent with the evidence briefly outlined above. The exact details and consequences of that status may never be fully resolved, although excavation (on a sufficient scale) of selected areas within the fort and inside the civil settlement would undoubtedly illuminate some of the problems summarised here, relating both to the general status and function of such settlements in the north, as well as the specific questions relating to Ribchester.

I am indebted to Dr D.Breeze and Mr R.C.Turner who took great pains in reading a draft manuscript of this chapter. This work has benefited considerably from their valuable advice and comments; its imperfections, however, remain the sole responsibility of the author.

BIBLIOGRAPHY AND ABBREVIATIONS

Birley R. 1973   Civilians on the Roman frontier, Newcastle.

Birley R. 1977   Vindolanda: A Roman frontier post on Hadrian's Wall, London.

Blagg T.F.C. & King A.C. 1984   Military and civilian in Roman Britain BAR British Ser., 136, Oxford.

Branigan K. 1980   Rome and the Brigantes: the impact of Rome on northern England, Sheffield.

Breeze D. 1982   'Demand and supply on the northern frontier', in P.Clack & S.Hazelgrove (eds.), 1982, 148-165.

Breeze D. & Dobson, B., 1976   Hadrians Wall, London.

Breeze D. & Dobson B. 1985   'Roman military deployment in North England', Britannia, 16, 1-21.

Bu'lock J.D. 1961   'The Bronze Age in the North West', Trans. Lancashire Cheshire Antiq. Soc., 71, 1-41.

Burgess C. 1980   The Age of Stonehenge, London.

Casey J. 1982   'Civilian and soldier - Friends, Romans, Countrymen?', in P.Clack & S.Hazelgrove (eds.), 1982, 123-132.

Chapman J.C. & Mytum H.C. 1983   Settlement in North Britain 1000 B.C.-A.D.1000. BAR British Ser., 118, Oxford.

Charlesworth D. 1964.   'Excavation at Kirkby Thore, 1964', Trans. Cumb. & Westmorland Ant. & Arch. Soc., N.S., 65, 426-427.

Clack P. & Hazelgrove S. 1982   Rural settlement in the Roman North, CBA Group 3, Durham.

Collingwood R.G. & Richmond I.A. 1969   The archaeology of Roman Britain. revised edition, London.

Collingwood R.G. & Wright R.P. 1965   The Roman inscriptions of Britain. I. Inscriptions on stone. Oxford.

Crickmore J. 1984   Romano-British urban defences. BAR British Ser., 126, Oxford.

Dore J.
& Greene K. 1977

Roman pottery studies in Britain and beyond. BAR Suppl. Ser., 30, Oxford.

Edwards B.J.N. 1972

Ribchester. National Trust.

Edwards B.J.N.
& Webster P.V. 1985

Ribchester excavations part 1. Excavations within the Roman Fort 1970-1980. Cardiff.

Evans J.G. et.al. 1975

The effect of man on the landscape: the highland zone. C.B.A. Research Report No.11. London.

Frere S.S. 1967

Britannia. London.

Frere S.S. 1975

'The origin of small towns', in W.Rodwell & T.Rowley (eds.), 1975, 4-8.

Frere S.S. 1984

'British urban defences in earth-work', Britannia, 15, 63-74.

Gibbons P. forthcoming

'Kirkby Thore: trial trenches 1983', Trans. Cumb. & Westmorland Ant. & Arch. Soc. N.S.

Gillam J.P. 1970

Types of Roman coarse pottery vessels in northern Britain. 3rd Edition, Newcastle.

Gillam J.P. 1976

'Coarse fumed ware in North Britain and beyond', Glasgow Arch. J., 4, 57-80.

Godwin E.G. 1979

Ribchester bath-house: an interim report of the 1978 excavations, Lanc. County Mus. Service, Preston.

Hallam J. 1970

'The Prehistory of Lancashire', Arch. J., 127, 232-237.

Hartley B.R. 1980

'The Brigantes and the Roman army', in K.Branigan (ed.), 1980, 2-7.

Hartley K.F.
& Webster P.V. 1973

'Romano-British pottery kilns near Wilderspool', Arch. J., 130, 77-103.

Higham N.J. 1982

'The Roman impact upon rural settlement in Cumbria', in P.Clack & S.Hazelgrove (eds.), 105-122.

Hind J.F. 1977

'The Genounian part of Britain', Britannia, 7, 229 -234.

Holder P.A. 1982

The Roman army in Britain. London.

Hunter J.K. et.al. 1971

'Recent excavations at the Slack Roman Fort near Huddersfield', Yorks. Arch. J., 42, 74-97.

Johnson S. 1984 'Vici in lowland Britain', in W.Rodwell & T.Rowley (eds.), 1975, 75–84.

Jones G.D.B. 1984 'Becoming different without knowing it – the role and development of vici', in T.F.C.Blagg & A.C.King (eds.), 1982, 75–92.

Jones G.D.B. & Walker J. 1983 'Either side of Solway', in J.C.Chapman & H.C.Mytum (eds.), 1983, 185-204.

Jones M.J. 1977 'Archaeological work at Brough under Stainmore, 1971-2', **Trans. Cumb. & Westmorland Ant. & Arch. Soc. N.S.**, 77, 17-47.

Manning W.H. 1975 'Economic influences on land use in the military areas of the highland zone during the Roman period', in J.G.Evans, et al. (eds.), 1975, 112-116.

Manning W.H. 1981 **Report on the excavations at Usk 1965-1976: The fortress excavations 1968-1971.** Cardiff.

Margary I.D. 1967 **Roman roads in Britain.** revised ed. London.

Millett M. 1984 'Forts and the origins of towns: cause or effect?', in T.F.C.Blagg & A.C.King (eds.), 1982, 65-74.

Philp B. 1981 **The excavation of the Roman forts of the Classis Britannica at Dover, 1970-1977.** Kent Monograph Series No.2.

Potter T.W.P. 1979 **Romans in North-West England. Cumb. & Westmorland Antiq. & Arch. Soc. Res. ser.**, 1. Kendal.

Radley J. 1966 'A Bronze Age ring-work on Totley Moor and other Bronze Age ring-works in the Pennines', **Arch. J.**, 123, 1-26.

Ramm H. 1978 **The Parisi.** London.

RIB see Collingwood & Wright 1965.

Reynolds M. & Barber J. 1984 'Analytical excavation', **Antiquity**, 58, 95-102.

Richmond I.A. 1945 'The Sarmatae, Bremetennacum Veteranorum and the Regio Bremetennacensis', **J. Roman Studies**, 35, 15-29.

Rodwell W. **Small towns of Roman Britain.** BAR British

& Rowley T. (eds.) 1975   Ser., 15, Oxford.

Salway P. 1965   The frontier people of Roman Britain. Cambridge.

Salway P. 1980   'The vici: urbanisation in the North', in K.Branigan (ed.), 1980, 8-17.

Salway P. 1981   Roman Britain. Oxford.

Simpson G. 1985   'Ribchester Roman fort: its historical outline', in B.J.N.Edwards & P.V.Webster (eds.), 1985, 9-19.

Sommer C.S. 1984   The military vici in Roman Britain. BAR British Ser.,129, Oxford.

Thompson F.H. 1965   Roman Cheshire. Chester.

Todd M. 1970   'The small towns of Roman Britain', Britannia, 1, 114-130.

Wacher J.S. 1974   The towns of Roman Britain. London.

Wacher J.S. 1975   'Village fortifications', in W.Rodwell & T.Rowley (eds.), 51-52.

Webster P.V. 1971   'Melandra Castle Roman Fort: excavations in the civil settlement 1966-1969', Derb.Arch. J., 91, 58-118.

Webster P.V. 1977   'Severn Valley Ware on the Antonine Frontier', in J.Dore & K.Greene (eds.), 1977, 163-176.

Welsby D.A. 1982   The Roman military defence of the British provinces in its Later phases. BAR British Ser., 101, Oxford.

Wilson D.R. 1984   'Defensive outworks of Roman forts in Britain', Britannia, 15, 51-61.

Printed by:

ABBEY BOOKBINDING & PRINTING Co.,
CARDIFF
Tel: (0222) 395882